In the Beginning, Middle, and End

A Screenwriter's Observations of
Life, Character, and God

Jaclyn Whitt

Faith & Family
Filmmakers
Association

Butterfly Books
Publishing

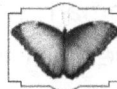

Want to get the insider look at one of Jaclyn's most well-loved scripts?

This is truly one you don't want to miss out on!

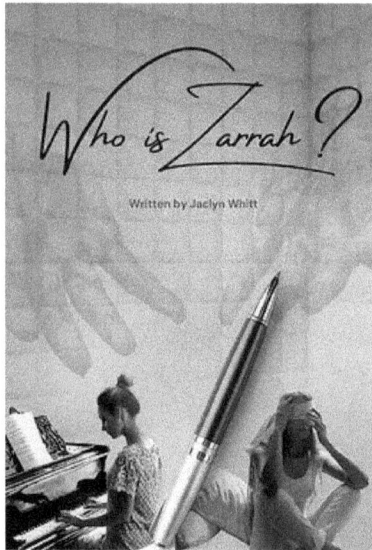

As my way of saying thank you for getting *In the Beginning, Middle, and End*, I'd like to give you this special gift sharing the journey for a woman who faces the ultimate quest in discovering who she really is.

Get this gift at: *jaclynwhitt.com/who-is-zarrah*

What Readers Have to Say:

In the Beginning, Middle, and End is not just a guide for writing but a guide for life. This book not only helped me to understand how to make my scripts and stories more intentional and meaningful but also how to see my own life and journey as a story that is full of intention and purpose. I walked away from the book with a deeper love and respect for myself, my creator, and my creativity. How one book can make me grow emotionally, creatively, and spiritually is so inspiring. Jaclyn Whitt is not only a great screenwriter but an amazing author and inspiration! Will read it again and again!

~JD Creviston,
Comedian, Podcaster, Writer

This book confirms what I feel in my bones - that "we live in a love story set in war," (as John Eldredge says). It's so very validating and encouraging - and not just for writers, but for anyone with a pulse. I recommend it because it will help you navigate difficult relationships, call you deeper into your named identity and give you clarity as to the way things work in this dreadfully fallen, scandalously beautiful world. "In The Beginning, Middle and End" will inject supernatural hope into your soul... reminding us that the Author of all our stories loves every one of His works and would never abandon a single one without finishing what He started.

~Karthi Masters,
Writer, Storyteller, Certified Life Coach, Empty NEXTer.

In the Beginning, Middle, and End: A Screenwriter's Observations of Life, Character, and God

Copyright © 2024 Jaclyn Whitt

First Edition Published by Faith & Family Filmmakers Association in partnership with Butterfly Books Publishing

Cover Design by Rob of I Love My Cover Designs
Interior Design and Typesetting by Butterfly Books Publishing
Edited by Stephanie Grohall

ISBN (paperback): 979-8-9905662-4-8

Printed in the United States of America.

www.jaclynwhitt.com

Table of Contents

I'd like to dedicate this book to my parents, Ron and Mary-Jo Redlin, and my husband, Geoffrey Whitt, for being my biggest supporters and encouragers to becoming a writer.

Foreword

Have you ever felt like you are just a character in a lifelong story being told? Maybe that's because you are.

Screenwriter Jaclyn Whitt takes her experiences as a storyteller and uses them to show your part in your own story.

For example, she explains the function of obstacles and tests in movies, and then applies those lessons so you can identify the purpose of the obstacles in your own life. Or, how figuring out what genre you are currently living through can help you get past your current hardships (ie. maybe you are in a comedy, and your struggles are the comic bits leading to personal growth). Or, how knowing that your Author (God) is writing your story with the ending in mind puts life's trials into perspective.

This deeply personal and highly accessible book is chockful of such lessons; and each chapter is very applicable to your own journey from fade-in to restored balance.

I met Jaclyn through her podcast, as a guest. Our tastes and outlook meshed instantly. We both saw story as something more than an outline for entertainment; we saw story as something practical and applicable to life.

This meeting led to me sitting in on a table read of one of her screenplays (*Who is Zarrah?* – excerpts found in this book), which led to additional conversations – notes, responses, and more on how the stories are not just stories.

I was then asked to be an early reader of this book. I expected a screenwriter's how-to, a textbook for the budding writer to map out the steps of creating a script. And that is in there, sure; but what this book is truly about is how we live our lives.

We both agree that stories are practical to life; Jaclyn goes on to show how *storytelling* principles are also practical and applicable.

Here's the thing: God put in us the way to tell and receive stories. And that implant is meant to help us understand the story He is creating with us.

I've written my own book (in the publication pipeline as of this writing).

In an introductory chapter, I wrote this:

"The universal elements that our souls long for when we hear "Once upon a time..." are more than flights of escape: they are nuanced elements that draw us to a home we don't yet know. They give us ears to hear -- even when we don't quite understand all we hear. The central thesis of this book is simple: God has hardwired in us how to tell and receive stories in the hopes that in understanding story, we might better understand Him."

Jaclyn's book articulates that very idea. Each element of storytelling informs us about the great Storyteller. These glimpses into the process give us the tools to understanding our own plot, role, goals, and obstacles.

Want to know how you fit in your own story?

Read Jacyln Whitt's *In the Beginning, Middle, and End*.

-Sean Gaffney
Professor of Media and Screenwriting
Asbury University
Screenwriting Credits include:
Veggie Tales
The Veggie Tales Show
Superbook
In-Lawfully Yours
Not Your Romeo and Juliet

Introduction

Do you ever feel like a character in a movie? Things happen all around you that are out of your control, and you wonder what on earth the writer is doing. Why does it sometimes feel like life is progressing smoothly and other times it feels like you keep bumping up against the same brick wall? Are there lessons we're supposed to be learning? Could there actually be a purpose to everything happening around us, and to us?

Hey, thanks for being here! We're going to take a deep dive into my ideas, theories and observations as a created being and as a creator myself. I'm looking forward to sharing my heart, history, and storytelling techniques with you.

But, before we dive into the plethora of thoughts that my brain has finally been able to articulate, I need to explain my format for the book. Since I'm a screenwriter, I've taken the liberty to include scripts in this book. Most chapters will have a segment of a script in order to assist in making my point. If you've never read a screenplay before, fear not, I'm going to give you a crash course in how to read one. But first...

!!! SPOILER ALERT !!!

READ THIS BEFORE YOU READ FURTHER

As part of using my scripts as examples, there is one script where I give away the ending. If you are someone who'd rather read the script first, and then read the chapter that dives into its ending, you're welcome to do so. The script is called *Who is Zarrah?* The most common response I get from readers is that it's a page turner and a mind-bender. Hopefully, I'll be able to produce it someday.

As my gift to you as a reader of this book, you can read the script at: *jaclynwhitt.com/who-is-zarrah*.

If you're unfamiliar with screenplays, here are some tips to help you read and interpret the scripts.

Overview:

The first thing you'll notice when you look at a script is that the margins are all over the place. That's because different elements have their own place on the page. Once you understand it, you'll realize it actually makes it easier to read. The other thing you'll notice is that there's a lot of white on the page. It'll take about 1 – 2 minutes to read each page of a screenplay.

Terminology and Function:

Scene Headings:

INT. means "Interior"
EXT. means "Exterior"

You'll see this at the start of every scene as it will clarify where the scene takes place. It'll always be either inside (INT.) or outside (EXT.).

For example:

```
INT. CAFÉ - DAY
```

That means the scene takes place inside the café during daytime. Simple! The second part of the scene heading states the location and the last part states the general time. (Typically, DAY or NIGHT.) If you see it say (CONTINUOUS) it means that the character moved from one location to another, but it's meant to appear as a seamless movement, like when a person walks through a door to another room; new location, but continuous action.

Action Lines:

The line that follows the scene heading will be an action line which explains what you'd see on the screen. It doesn't get into a lot of detail, but it gives enough information for you to understand the story and allows your imagination to fill in the rest.

Sometimes, you might see a word capitalized. You don't need to worry about that. Since a screenplay is a blueprint for the entire production, there are cues for various other roles to take note of. For example, when a character is first introduced to the story, or when there's a sound that's not included in dialogue. These are details for casting and sound editing.

Character Names, Parentheticals, and Dialogue:

The capitalized names in the center of the page indicate that the dialogue that follows is spoken by that character.

For example:

```
                    JENNY
          (whining)
     Can we just get to the point already?
```

Jenny is the character speaking and that's what she said, and how she said it. (She'd really like for me to finish explaining how to read a script so we get on to the fun stuff.)

Whatever note is made within the parenthesis, it's a clarification of how the character delivers the line. It might be with an emotion, but it might indicate who they're speaking to if it's not already obvious within the context of the scene. It might also indicate something in the scene that the character is commenting on. These aren't used very often, so if you don't understand what it means, you can probably ignore it and keep reading. You'll figure out what's happening soon enough.

(V.O.) and Other Extensions:

Sometimes a character is speaking, but there's something different about how we hear them. (V.O.) means Voiceover. That's when the audience hears the dialogue, but none of the characters in the scene do. It's like we're inside the character's head, or it's a narration.

(O.S.) and (O.C.) mean almost the same thing. "Off Screen" and "Off Camera". There's someone speaking within the scene, but they're not visible to the audience.

(ON PHONE) means exactly what it says; the voice is coming through the phone. There are a few others, but they're easily understood. Take a look:

```
              REPORTER (ON RADIO)
    This just in, "how to read a script"
    isn't so complicated after all.
```

See? You got this.

Cut-off's and Trail-off's:

When you see a double dash (--) in dialogue, it means that the line was cut-off abruptly. When you see an ellipsis (...), it means that the dialogue trailed off.

The Hero:

Many authors will refer to their main character as the "main character" or "protagonist". They're not wrong. These are completely accurate terms to describe the main character/protagonist. But we screenwriters often refer to that character as the "hero". This doesn't refer to superheroes, or triumphant heroes, it's not gender specific and it's not to say that the character starts out as a hero, but rather that we, the writer, believe in the character's potential from the start. (Plus, "hero" sounds more exciting.) So, when I refer to "the hero" I'm just referring to the main character of the plot, but in a way that's more fun and standard to the film industry.

If you want to learn more about how to read or write a script, I offer online workshops and classes throughout the year. Visit my website to learn more at: *faffassociation.com.*

And that's it! Happy reading. I pray this book blesses you.

Chapter 1
How it All Begins

In the beginning... no wait! In the end... YES! Let's start at the end. That is, in fact, where it all begins.

Writing with purpose requires a goal. A writer must write with the end in mind. The question I ask myself as a screenwriter is, "What lesson do I want my hero to learn?"

There will come a time in which it will become clear whether he's going to learn the lesson or not. It will come after he's been given all of the tools and opportunity to grow. Then, and only then, will it rest on his shoulders to choose growth. And he will reap the consequences of his choice, one way or the other.

Endings can bring satisfaction, closure, and beauty. They can also bring sadness, revelation, and a warning. What makes a good ending good, even if things didn't turn out for the hero the way we'd hoped, is justice. Does the ending do the journey justice? Does the journey do the ending justice? Can we see how that conclusion came about? Or was there a surprise detail that came out of nowhere and fixed everything?

Cop-out endings lack satisfaction, not only because it lacks creativity, but because the human experience exists in the realm of natural consequences. The Author of our existence rarely swoops in to fix things, despite our incessant pleas for him to do so. However, in his justice, he affords us the tools to learn and grow. He takes us on a journey filled with learning opportunities and then allows us to choose how it ends. Do we embrace the lesson or reject it? So, let's venture into endings because there's a lot to learn about life, character arcs, and God.

Get ready for the spoiler I warned you about! (If you skipped the Introduction and started with Chapter 1, I encourage you to go back and read the Introduction first... don't say I didn't warn you.)

The following scenes are an example of a woman who's had her world turned up-side-down so much that she doesn't even know which version of herself is real anymore. All she knows is that she hates herself for something she did as a child. Her regret is eating her up inside. At this point in the story, she's been given all of the information and opportunities to figure out the truth and to forgive herself, yet she still has not embraced it. But the final test is where the hero comes face to face with the very thing she's been avoiding which can no longer be avoided. Her rock bottom was lower than she could've ever imagined, only to lead her to her biggest and final test.

Climax scene from Who is Zarrah, written by Jaclyn Whitt:

INT. PSYCH WARD ZARRAH'S CELL - DAY

Zarrah sits on her bed while Nurse Giovani checks her blood pressure.

> ZARRAH
> Grace says I have to forgive myself.
> But, I... I can't. I won't.

                    NURSE GIOVANI
          You won't forgive a toddler?

                    ZARRAH
          I hate her... me.

                    NURSE GIOVANI
          Hmm...

Nurse Giovani considers his next statement as he
packs up his equipment.

                    NURSE GIOVANI
          Zarrah, now that your memory has
          returned, you're coming to the end of
          your time here.

                    ZARRAH
          What do you mean? Where am I going?

Nurse Giovani pushes his equipment out of the room.

                    NURSE GIOVANI
          That depends.

He exits and closes the door behind him.

Zarrah stands, disturbed and confused.

                    ZARRAH
          On what? Wait!

Zarrah rushes through the door...

INT. PSYCH WARD ROOM WITH PADDED WALLS - CONTINUOUS

Zarrah rushes through the door into the room with
white padded walls and tiny-hand blood-stains on
them.

She stops, stunned.

She turns back, but the door is gone. It's the room from her original nightmare.

She processes what's happening.

She hears a SNIFF behind her.

Zarrah turns to see 3-year-old Zarrah, with blood on her hands and blood specks on her face, CRYING and afraid.

Zarrah stares at the girl, keeping her distance.

The toddler starts to shake her hand, like she's trying to shake off the blood.

Zarrah looks down to see her own hand shaking at her side.

3-year-old Zarrah WHIMPERS.

Zarrah slowly approaches the toddler and kneels down in front of her.

                    3-YEAR-OLD ZARRAH
          I want Mommy and Daddy.

                    ZARRAH
          I miss them so much.

3-year-old Zarrah tries to wipe the blood off her hands, then holds them out to Zarrah as if to ask for help.

Zarrah reaches toward the toddler, then pulls back, seeing her own hands covered in blood.

Zarrah glances between her hands and the toddler's.

She collapses beside the little girl. They stare at each other through tears for a moment.

Finally, Zarrah softens and pulls the toddler into her embrace, releasing years of self-hatred.

                    ZARRAH
          I'm sorry. I forgive you.

After a few moments, Zarrah looks at the toddler to see the blood gone from her hands and face.

Her own hands are clean again.

She wipes a tear from the toddler's face.

The toddler wipes a tear from Zarrah's face.

                    ZARRAH
          Let's go home.

Zarrah stands and takes the toddler's hand.

The room seamlessly transforms into a white, boundary-less space.

They walk together into a fog.

Ahh... forgiveness and reconciliation with one's self. What a beautiful moment. A satisfying ending to a disturbing journey. Not all beauty is birthed from pain, but some of the most beautiful moments are earned through excruciating journeys.

Zarrah's journey includes the realization that she has caused the death of her own parents when she was a toddler. This revelation comes about while she pursues counseling for her mental illness and psychosis that causes her to question her own identity, and the identities of everyone around her. In the scene where she comes face to face with her toddler self, she has to choose how to respond. What you also need to understand is that her sanity hangs in the balance.

Everything that could be beautiful and wonderful in her life is waiting for her on the other side of her character arc. It's a bridge that no one can cross for her. She has to choose it for herself.

In the beginning, as I was developing this story of beauty from agony, I had to consider what it would take to get Zarrah's attention enough to force her to deal with her perception of truth. I understood the stakes if she didn't and I also knew how stubborn she'd be during the process. When Zarrah was just an idea in my mind, I was thinking through her journey. It looked a little something like this...

INT. BEDROOM - NIGHT

JACLYN, 30's, a full-time caregiver and aspiring screenwriter, stares blankly at the ceiling while thoughts turn in her head.

> JACLYN (V.O.)
> Okay, she's got a test coming. She's going to meet her own self. Will she forgive and embrace her inner child so she can reintegrate as one person, or will she reject her younger self and remain fractured? Good test. I like it. It's messy.

Jaclyn smiles to herself, then looks over at her husband.

He SNORES without a care in the world.

> JACLYN (V.O.)
> Must be nice.

Let's get into the inevitable test. Before I sit down to write a script, I know exactly how it's going to end. The final showdown is already clear in my mind. I know my hero and the specific character flaw that will be tested throughout the story. All of it will lead to one final moment of decision. My job as the writer is to get my hero ready for THAT test. The Bible says that God knows the end from the beginning. That's exactly what a writer needs to know as well. (Surprise, surprise; the Author of the greatest stories ever told knows a thing or two about storytelling.)

As a screenwriter, the god of the story's universe, I can't communicate directly with the characters the way they can communicate directly with each other. However, my job as the screenwriter is to give my hero every opportunity to arc. In fact, it is my responsibility to do so. The only way to do that is to interject obstacles, introduce new characters, and create circumstances to direct them toward choosing the path I want them to take.

To be fair, I always give them the opportunity to walk away from their flaw up front, but if they don't take it (which, in movies, they won't, or there'd be no story), then I have the right to present consequences and obstacles. (Remember the part about justice? If I didn't give my character the opportunity to choose to overcome their flaw upfront, the journey would seem unjust.) Each time my character fails to grow, I must increase the stakes and the obstacles.

For these stubborn characters, they end up eventually coming to a low point we call the "crisis" or the "dark night of the soul". This is the moment where they're exhausted by their journey, they've not yet figured out an answer, they're ready to give-up (potentially even on life itself), and they long for their old life. The problem is that they've gone through too much to be the person they used to be, thus going back is not an option.

Sound familiar? I'm sure I'm not the only one who has found herself in a cycle of repeating the same lesson over and over until she finally learns. Think back to some of the hardest lessons you've had to learn. You probably had opportunities to learn the easy way and chose not to. (I hope I'm not just baring my soul to perfect people who never had to learn the hard way.)

So, there my hero is, in this moment where he feels like he can't go back and he doesn't know how to go forward. This is what it takes sometimes to bring us to the point of surrender. But this isn't a place that allows one to linger for long. A decision must be made. And the hero is the one who makes it. Either he will choose to grow by embracing the lessons learned in his past, or he will harden his heart and dig his heels into his flaw.

"Wait, what's this 'lessons learned' stuff? I thought you said you failed to learn, that's why you're in a crisis," you ask?

Good question. In order to give my hero an opportunity to "learn while he's refusing to learn," I give him a parallel journey. Here, he's able to more easily understand the principles he needs in order to achieve his character arc. Yes, two journeys at the same time, but one is more obvious and simple to understand.

For example, if a teen is in rebellion and headed for a life that'll land him in jail or the grave, I can create an opportunity for him to be on a sports team. There, he'll struggle and fail until he learns how to submit to authority, be a team player, take responsibility, develop resiliency and embrace the satisfaction of giving his all. After learning those skills there, he's able to take those same principles and apply it to his personal life and relationships. And it is in fact these principles that he'll need in order to overcome his inevitable test.

As a screenwriter, I specialize in subtext, but for the sake of clarity, I'm going to write some "on the nose" statements.

One of my biggest lessons learned is the realization that not all trials are of the devil. For real, friends. Sometimes, it's God who flips life on its head. But don't take this as bad news. It's actually amazingly wonderful news because while the enemy might be out to get you, God is out to get you ready. Whatever obstacles he creates are specifically and strategically targeted to get you ready for something you can't see coming. It might be years down the road before any of it finally makes sense to you, if it ever does.

As I grew into becoming a screenwriter and realized that I actually get to play god, I began to understand God beyond Father, Savior, King, and Friend. I began to understand his creative side which allowed me to change my expectations. Instead of asking God, "Why?!" when things went wrong, I began asking, "What am I supposed to be learning here?" And I'd open my eyes in my life and try to observe it objectively.

Strangely enough, there were times where I could immediately see what I needed to learn, but I was too stubborn to submit to the lesson without having to take that journey of obstacles. And sometimes, I ended up on the journey in order to learn the lessons, because while I may have known what I needed to address and was willing to do so, I didn't always know how to change. However, that particular type of journey comes with a lot fewer frustrations. It's still difficult, but because I was able to understand that the struggles of the journey came with purpose, I was able to embrace them.

"Wait, I thought we were talking about endings."

That's correct. Endings come with a new perspective. We can see where we are and look back at how we got there. We can see that everything led us to exactly this place. If a hero gets to the end of his well-earned character arc and doesn't take a moment to reflect on the journey, we can't know for sure if he's internalized it. I think that the more we analyze our lives and look back to see where we were and where we are, we can thank our Author despite the tough times and necessary sacrifices along the way.

The Author of life is also the Author of love. So, if my Author decides to place or permit trials in my life, I choose to trust and embrace the journey. I can't tell you how many times I learned a lesson just in time for it to really matter! Which brings us to the best part. After we've faced our inevitable test and crossed the character arc bridge, there is a beautiful reward. Freedom.

When we look back, we can see how much that character flaw was holding us in bondage. But now, on the other side of the learning process, we get to experience life with our newly earned character strength. It doesn't fix all of our problems, there may still be consequences that play out, but the weight of that particular flaw has been lifted. And as this process repeats over and over in our lives, we move from glory to glory.

Chapter 2
The Author's Investment
in the Journey

If that is how God clothes the grass of the field,
which is here today and tomorrow is thrown into the fire,
will he not much more clothe you... Matthew 6:30

It might seem obvious to say this, but in any story's development, the person who is the most invested in how it plays out is the writer. The writer obsesses over the story, the characters, and the plot points until he's satisfied that the character is the right character for the plot and that the plot is the right plot for the character.

In the scene below, the story has just jumped forward 11 years. In the opening pages, Jackson and Danita were in high school and clearly crazy about each other. But they each had big dreams of pursuing music and went their separate ways after school without confessing their feelings for one another. Here, we get a clear picture of where Jackson's at in his life, as well as a glimpse into what he needs to get back on track.

SCENE FROM JACKSON AND DANITA, WRITTEN BY JACLYN
WHITT

INT. BAR - NIGHT

Jackson sits at the bar, staring into space, swirling
a drink in his cup. The twinkle in his eye is long
gone.

A FLIRTATIOUS WOMAN, 28 approaches him.

                    FLIRTATIOUS WOMAN
          Mind if I join you?

Jackson reluctantly turns to her without a response.

                    FLIRTATIOUS WOMAN
          I saw you sitting here alone...

Jackson looks her up and down, unimpressed.

                    FLIRTATIOUS WOMAN
          I'm Angie.

She extends her hand.

                    JACKSON
          Not my type.

Jackson returns to drinking.

                    FLIRTATIOUS WOMAN
          Excuse me?

                    JACKSON
          You're not my type.

                    FLIRTATIOUS WOMAN
          You don't even know me.

                    JACKSON
          You're beautiful. You take care of
          yourself. Yet, you're clearly needy
          for attention.

                 FLIRTATIOUS WOMAN
          Wha...

                    JACKSON
          Drama.

Jackson downs his drink, ignoring Angie. Angie
watches in shock, then shakes her head and walks off.

MOSES, 40, a bartender, approaches.

                     MOSES
          Smooth, bro.

                    JACKSON
          I dated a woman just like her. Never.
          Again.

Jackson's PHONE RINGS. He pulls his cell out of his
pocket and checks the caller ID.

Jackson groans and reluctantly answers.

                    JACKSON
          Yeah. Yeah, I... I'm sick. I'm at home
          in bed. Sorry. No, for real, I'm,
          uh... I'm watching a movie... What?

Jackson searches the room one way, then the other.

MAC, 48, Jackson's blue-collar boss stands at the end
of the bar on his cell.

Jackson scolds himself and Mac approaches.

                          MAC
        I told you if you played hooky again,
        I'd can you.

                        JACKSON
        C'mon Boss, I had a bad night last
        night.

                          MAC
        Forget it. I'm through giving you
        chances. You're fired.

Mac turns to leave, then turns back.

                          MAC
        You know, you could've at least had
        the sense not to come to my bar.

                        JACKSON
        Your bar?

                          MAC
        You know I come here every Thursday
        after work.

                        JACKSON
        It's Thursday?

Mac scowls at Jackson and storms off.

Jackson turns to Moses and motions for another drink.

                        MOSES
            (chuckling)
        You're a real piece a work.

Moses pours Jackson another drink.

                        JACKSON
        You should see me on Tuesdays.

Jackson gets a PHONE call. He looks at the caller ID: "UNKNOWN NUMBER".

                    JACKSON
     Hello.

                    DANITA (ON PHONE)
               (chipper)
     You never called.

Jackson pauses and looks at the number.

                    DANITA (ON PHONE)
     Jackson, you there?

                    JACKSON
     Ah-- wha-- yeah. Yeah, I'm... Danita?

                    DANITA (ON PHONE)
     I know it's out of the blue. But, I
     was just wondering why you're not
     going to Laura's wedding.

                    JACKSON
     Laura's wedding?

                    DANITA (ON PHONE)
     Don't play dumb. She told me she
     invited you and you declined. Look, I
     know you've probably got this amazing,
     busy life, but I'm asking you to
     please reconsider. I'm playing a song
     for their first dance and, well... It
     could really use a trumpet solo.

Jackson pretends to pound his head on the bar
counter.

Moses watches, amused.

                    JACKSON
          Uh... look, Danita, I... I already
          declined attending, so...

INT. DANITA'S HOME - SAME

Danita paces, biting her lip, but speaks confidently.

                    DANITA
          You can come as my plus one.

INTERCUT BETWEEN JACKSON AND DANITA

                    JACKSON
          Ugh... Danny...

Jackson rubs his eyes, trying to sober up.

                    DANITA
          You don't need to answer right now. I
          mean, you're probably gonna need to
          think about it. Maybe cancel a gig or
          something...

                    JACKSON
          I don't. I don't play anymore.

                    DANITA
          What? But...

                    JACKSON
          I can't do it.

                    DANITA
          Well... The wedding's not for a few
          weeks. I can send you the music and
          you can practice. We could meet up the
          day before to rehearse--

                    JACKSON
          You're not listening. I'm not a
          musician anymore.

                          22

                         DANITA
          It's one song at our friends' wedding.

Jackson leans his head into his hand like the
conversation is causing him physical pain.

                         DANITA
          Come on. It'll be like old times.
          Please? For me? I wrote the song
          myself... for you.

Jackson melts.

Danita catches her vulnerability and covers it.

                         DANITA
          Okay, it's not for you, it's... It's
          for you to play... Like how you wrote
          songs for me to sing.

                         JACKSON
             Did you really write it for me?

                         DANITA
          Well, there's this trumpet solo I keep
          hearing in my head and, um...

Danita scolds her horrible cover-up.

                         DANITA
          Look, I know you're probably gonna
          want to make some suggestions and
          change some lyrics or whatever, which,
          I mean, cool, I guess. I just want it
          to be good and--

                         JACKSON
          I'll think about it.

                         DANITA
                 (forcing confidence)
          Ya, you will.

Jackson GROANS.

                         DANITA
               Hey, you said it. I'll take it! Let me
               know soon, okay?

Danita hangs up and exhales heavily.

END INTERCUT WITH DANITA

Jackson hangs up.

Moses saunters over.

                         MOSES
               She must be something. Ain't no girl I
               seen ever get to you like that.

                         JACKSON
               I have only two regrets with women.

                         MOSES
               She messed you up, good, huh?

                         JACKSON
               Nah... I was the one who messed that
               one up.

Jackson pulls out his wallet and starts counting.

                         MOSES
               Ah... The one that got away.

                         JACKSON
               Something like that.

Jackson gets frustrated with counting and just leaves
it all on the bar.

Jackson exits. Moses gladly counts the cash.

Jackson has not only lost his way, but we get a hint that he's been through some stuff and has decided that giving up is his best option. So, how does a writer get a hero, who's given up on life, to get up off his bar stool and care about something? We pull out the big guns. We know what motivates him, what he can't say no to, and what can find the cracks in the wall. Danita is Jackson's kryptonite and his biggest regret. Because of this, I know that she's the one who can remind him of who he really is. I can use her to redirect Jackson back to the path of becoming all that he could be.

When you watch a movie, you're going to watch a character who has a specific flaw that he needs to overcome and then see the evidence of how invested the writer is in finding a way to help him achieve it. The writer will put the hero into some really creative situations. Honestly, whatever it takes to get my characters to figure it out, I'll do it. If it means I need to put them in danger, I will. If it means I need to take relationships away from them, I will. Do they hate me for it? Absolutely. But after they've grown, they're able to look back and find meaning in the journey.

Since I get to play god, I get to create a world, create the rules of the world, and create the characters who'll exist in that world. Many times, it's easy to just borrow from the world we live in and copy/paste all the same rules; laws of physics, time, space, architecture, etc. But I have the freedom to switch things up if I want. I can have characters who fly or who have deep thoughts that cause everyone in the scene to burst out in song. I can set it on a different planet with characters who aren't even human. I can make animals talk. So, where do I begin?

First, I have to ask myself what story I want to tell. Then, I have to figure out which world fits best to tell that story. I need to decide on the purpose of the story and the major dramatic question. The major dramatic question (MDQ) is what drives the story forward and it's how we know when it's over. The MDQ is basically this:

Will he _____ in order to _____ before _____?

What is the goal of the character? Why does the goal matter? And what are the stakes?

Here's an example of an MDQ from the greatest story ever told: Will Jesus live a sinless life in order for his death to cover the sins of humanity before humans are separated from God and damned to hell for eternity?

If I want to write a screenplay that has legs, has a chance of being produced, and will draw an audience, then I must have direction in the story. That's just good writing. Next, I need to create an adversary. That's right. I create the adversary.

I don't just create a character who needs to learn something, I also create a character who is whole-heartedly invested in preventing them from doing so. The adversary will sabotage the hero's efforts and do everything within their power to stop the hero from achieving success. And they have enough power to do it. It's only when the hero overcomes their flaw that they have what they need to overcome the adversary. The hero sees the adversary as a problem they'd be better off without.

But I, the writer, consider the adversary to play an integral role in the story. I use this character to get my hero's attention. Did you catch that? I use the adversary for my own purposes. The adversary is a benefit to me as the writer because I use him to put pressure on my hero to try harder, care deeper, and to push him out of his comfort zone.

Does my hero hate that an adversary is causing such havoc in his life? Yes. Yes, he does. Do I care that my hero is suffering because of it? Yes, but if I don't get my hero ready, he'll absolutely fail his test when it comes.

My number one priority is to create sufficient opportunity for my hero to achieve his character arc. If I fail to give the character an appropriate amount of opportunity to grow, because I don't want him to suffer, then I'm setting him up for failure and his suffering will be even greater in the end. Does he have any awareness or appreciation for this process that I'm putting him through? Absolutely not. He's completely unaware that I'm so deeply invested in his journey or that I'm doing everything in my power to get him ready for a big test in his future. But whether he would love me or hate me for it, I'm still fully invested in his life.

My job is to write a story that features a world I imagined with characters I created. If I've done it well, the audience forgets about me because they're so deeply drawn into the story. But, while I remain invisible, I am on every page. My plot connects and weaves like a dance. I set the tone, the pace, and the goal while I humbly remain anonymous. However, those who know my work, recognize it when they read it. My voice as a writer points to the story, but it's still my voice and my story. The same is true for our Author. While He may be invisible, he is revealed on every page of the story of our lives. And those who know His work can recognize it when they see it.

One of the most powerful revelations I've had about our Author by becoming one myself, is understanding that God reverse engineers our story. He's not just dealing with each day as it plays out. Rather, he's determining our steps based on where he's already decided we'll end up. He knows the test he has to get us ready for. He knows what we need to learn in order to prepare. He's not focussed on our survival, he's focussed on our success. His thoughts are not our thoughts because he knows all the factors. He knows what it takes to get us from who we are to who we need to be. And he's more invested in making it happen than we can fathom.

Chapter 3
The Author's Investment in Character Development

I praise you because I am fearfully and wonderfully made;
Psalm 139:14

Whether I'm writing a character for people to love, or love to hate, it's my responsibility to approach their character development in a way that allows him to live and behave from a place of authenticity. The character might lie, fake their way, or avoid facing the truth, but even that needs to come from a place of authenticity. I embrace them in this place, without expecting anything from them, and then proceed to take them on a journey.

To dig deeper into how I create my characters and bring them to life on the page, putting their own words into their mouths, let's zero in on how I approach the process. I take my responsibilities seriously and I'm committed to honoring their uniqueness. But, how do I fulfill such a commitment to my characters? With an incredible amount of hope, integrity, empathy, and love.

HOPE

No matter where my hero's journey starts, I need to greet him with hope in my heart. I know who he could become and I know that he's got a long way to go to get there. If I don't have an intense amount of hope for his future, I could grow weary and bitter trying to get him through the journey. The reality is that I know he's going to fail repeatedly, fight the process, dig his heels in, and blame me for his burdens.

What keeps me focused, determined, and unwavering in my pursuit, is hope; hope that he will eventually understand his need to change; hope that he will eventually submit to the journey and embrace it; hope that he will overcome his character flaw. Even in the times when I know he won't, because I know the end from the beginning, I maintain hope that he will come to a place where he has all the tools and understanding required to make the choice to overcome. At that point, I've done all I can. The rest is up to my hero's free will to choose.

I used to work for lawyers who practiced criminal law. One of these lawyers, after years of dealing with people with twisted, entitled attitudes, grew weary, frustrated, and pessimistic toward people. He had lost hope in people's ability to change and grow. While some might say that hope is a naive response to the world, "hope" is likely a big part of the childlike nature that Jesus was referring to when he said we must become like children in order to enter the Kingdom of Heaven. Children have hope despite what they see... until they've seen too much.

But the power of hope is stronger than many people give it credit for. Hope is what gets us through the tough times. And, in my twenties, it was when I lost hope that I began to struggle with suicidal ideation. When hope is lost, what's left? Can you imagine if God declared us a hopeless cause? The beautiful thing about our Author is that he's also the Author of hope. He demonstrated it by sending his Son to pay the ultimate price for sin that we committed, just for the hope that some would repent and embrace forgiveness so we could be reconciled to him. And it was hope that allowed Jesus to love and fellowship with Judas right to the end. He did everything he could to give Judas a chance to make a different choice, even to the point of calling him out and telling him that he was going to betray him. Hope is not just a nice idea. It's what allows us to fight for possibilities.

INTEGRITY

Before I explain "integrity", here's a sample of a script I wrote specifically to exemplify what happens when a writer writes WITHOUT integrity. (I almost wanted to let you figure it out for yourself, but I was afraid you might think this is some of my best work.)

```
INT. CAFE - NIGHT

POPPY, 16, street-smart, lonely, sweeps up the floor,
getting ready to close.

WENDY, 50, a former flower-power hippie, counts the
cash.

                    WENDY
        Poppy… there's over fifty dollars
        missing from the cash register.

                    POPPY
              (defensive)
        What? You think I took it? I wouldn't
        do that.
```

                    WENDY
        I'm not saying you took it. I just
        said it's missing. Do you have any
        idea how it might've happened?

                    POPPY
        Did you ask Jessica? Or just me?

                    WENDY
        Sunshine, I just discovered it myself.
        Of course, I didn't ask Jessica, yet.
        But, I will when I see her. Is
        everything alright?

                    POPPY
        None of your business.

Poppy puts the broom in the closet.

                    WENDY
        Poppy, you know you can talk to me.

                    POPPY
            (fighting tears)
        What do you care?

Wendy approaches Poppy and puts her arm around her.

                    WENDY
        I'm here for you.

Poppy bursts into tears.

                    POPPY
        My teacher said I missed too many days
        of school. I can't graduate. I'm going
        to be stuck here, working at a cafe my
        whole life. No offense.

                    WENDY
        I guess there's none taken. Would you
        like me to talk with your teacher?

```
                    POPPY
        Would you? Do you think it'd make a
        difference?

                    WENDY
        I'll try my best.

                    POPPY
        Wendy, there's something I need to
        tell you. I took the money. I was
        going to party with friends tonight.
        But, I don't want to anymore.

Poppy hands over the money.

                    WENDY
        Thanks for telling me the truth. I
        know you're not my own daughter, but I
        love you as if you were.

They embrace. All is well with the world.
```

Ugh... I want to gag. These characters are only saying and doing what I want them to, not what they would choose to do.

My characters need to think and speak for themselves. And that's good writing. In order to write well and do justice to my characters and their journey, I need to respect that my characters are different than I am. Sometimes, they know things I don't know. And I can't force them to be who they're not. Fun fact: Even though my character is different than I am, I know him better than he knows himself. I know what he needs even though he doesn't. And I don't have to wait for him to be on board with the plan for me to start the process.

By the way, if you didn't catch the double meaning in that last paragraph, that's how God works in our lives too. He's got a plan and he's going to pursue it whether we're on board with it or not. But he'll also respect our free will which will affect the journey and how it plays out. Just think about that for a bit.

Put yourself in the writer's shoes. How would you deal with an obstinate hero, knowing that if you don't give him the opportunity to grow, he's going to fail the final test unfairly and you'll be blamed because it was your responsibility to prepare him? My job as the writer is not to make a character say or do things, but to cause them to say or do things. I need to provide relationships and experiences that shape and mold them into who I'm calling them to be. And, by the way, writers don't give up on characters just because they don't want to go on the journey. We just get more creative with obstacles.

EMPATHY

Ask any writer and many will tell you that we feel what our characters feel. Despite knowing that they'll have a beautiful outcome, I often find myself in tears when my character's heart is breaking. I laugh when it's funny. Yes, yes, I know that I'm the one who wrote it, but I can imagine my character doing and saying things and, to me, they're alive in some sense. And I have to see them as alive in order for me to tell their story effectively.

Before I write it into an action line that tears begin to well in their eyes, I need to allow that emotion to emerge within me as I empathize with them. There are times when I'm just a mess of tears while I'm writing. As I write a heart-wrenching scene, despite knowing their backstory, their ending, their highs and lows, I'm absolutely in that moment with them. Even if I know that two pages later, I'm going to bust a gut laughing, as this difficult moment plays out, I'm not thinking about that other scene.

LOVE

Not all characters mature in the direction my heart longs for. In fact, some of my characters do some pretty awful things at times. But I don't abandon them. I know this is an expression of what's inside the character's heart and that it is my responsibility to address it. I won't walk away until the story is finished, even if they refuse to change their ways. I put the exact same amount of investment into providing opportunities for them to grow as with the stories where I know my character will achieve their character arc. For every one of my characters, I know all aspects of their life, past, present, future, and what could've been. And it's for that reason that I'm able to love them, even when they're stubborn, immature, acting like a jerk, etc.

My goal in the end is to give my character all the necessary tools that would allow him to make a conscious choice. If I don't, then the outcome would seem unfair and I would be accused of being a lazy and unjust writer. Instead of the audience realizing that the character missed their opportunity, they'll say it was poor writing and feel ripped-off. "He just needed more time," they could say. Or, "He wanted to change but the test was too hard. It wasn't fair." These accusations would mean that my process and conclusion for the story was unjust. Audiences don't appreciate a lack of justice in how a character's journey plays out, from the perspective of how it's written.

Alternatively, if a character achieves their character arc with basically no obstacles, we call it boring. There's something about struggling to achieve growth that we instinctively appreciate and value. And in order to create that balance, I must approach my character in love, even if that includes tough love.

The process of creating characters brings me joy and gives me a sense of purpose I can't explain. I think about so many details that don't even end up on the screen in the end, but I know those secret details because I know my characters. I don't just see my creations as interesting, flawed, or funny, I see them as children, adults, and in the moment. I'm not the only writer who tears up when sharing moments of the story that hit the hero hard. Quite often, that moment of discovery when the hero finally gets it, or when the wound is revealed, remains an emotional moment in the writer's heart. We were there with the hero through their journey of struggle, through their highs and lows, and when they hit that moment when they'll never be the same again. Every step of the way, we're right there with them. We're like proud parents, except that we're even more than that. We're their authors.

Your Author is also fully aware of your past, present, and future. He knows all your secrets. He was with you on your worst day. His heart broke with yours. He takes everything about you into consideration when setting you on a path.

God reveals his hope, integrity, empathy, and love for his people in the book of Exodus. First, empathy moves the heart of our Creator to respond to the cries of a nation in harsh slavery. After He reveals his power and faithfulness to Israel by bringing the plagues and deliverance, he states that he doesn't want to take the Israelites directly to their intended destination because the journey came with the threat of war.

Out of God's own integrity as an author, he wasn't going to expect them to respond in unnatural ways. God knew that war would be too much for them. They had been traumatized while in Egypt. Like a battered wife that was rescued from her abuser, Israel would need time to heal and gain confidence before facing conflict with another nation. As the Author, he chose the appropriate journey for his people. He worked with them, never giving up hope, knowing they would miss the mark multiple times. He knew their past, present, and future and loved them anyway. He journeyed with them and brought them into the promised land. He gave them victory over their enemies. By the way, this is the same God who has plans for your life.

I'm sure you've been told that God knows you better than you know yourself, but have you really thought that through? There's nothing you can do that will shock God. Regardless of whether he appreciates your choices or not, he's fully aware of your past, your future, your hurts, your dreams. He knows your wounds and the coping mechanisms you've established because of them. He knows how other people's actions affect you, what triggers you, what inspires you. He knows what brings you joy and he knows what pains you.

But he doesn't just know it all because he's an all-knowing God. He knows you because he's your Author. He won't miss, dismiss, or waste any of it. His goal is to bring beauty from ashes, give you the oil of joy to heal your mourning, a garment of praise instead of the spirit of heaviness, that you might be called a righteous tree planted by the Lord himself, that you may bring him glory. Isaiah 61:3 (paraphrased)

God is a master of character development. He's a loving Author who takes great pleasure and joy in watching us learn and grow. And he's more invested in our lives than any of us can fathom.

Chapter 4
Who's Who?

You're the only you there is.

When you watch movies, pay attention to the characters who are around the hero but don't seem to play a very significant role. A good writer will make these characters incredibly interesting, despite the fact that they don't get a lot of screen time. They might be more one-dimensional, but that dimension is well defined and more extreme. They might be eccentric, ornery, bubbly, unnecessarily depressed, annoying, arrogant, etc... These characters add energy and color to the story. But what about when they become real? Have you ever experienced people in your life that seem to be a little over-the-top? How do you deal with people who are just so "extra"?

A few years back, I bought a groupon for a relaxing massage session. I looked forward to it for weeks, but when I arrived, it was nothing like how I'd hoped. I'm the kind of person that likes to enjoy a massage in silence. I like to drift away into my own thoughts in a half-asleep state. However, this woman who was massaging me was the exact opposite. She loved to talk and kept engaging in conversation. She'd ask about me, and no matter what I responded, she'd say, "Oh, me too!" And proceeded to tell me her life story. It wasn't what I had planned, but it quickly became entertaining. The best part was her thick accent. (I love accents!)

"Do you have kids?" She asked.

"Yes. Two sons," I replied.

"Me, too! I have two sons. Both boys. What do you do for work?"

"I'm a fitness instructor," I responded.

"So am I! I teach on the second days..."

At first, I did my best to answer in a way that let the conversation fall flat, hoping to hint that I didn't really want to talk. But she wasn't picking up what I was putting down. In addition to that, she was quite the character. Since English wasn't her first language, she had unique ways of saying things. She also had a ton of energy and seemed to really want to make a connection.

The whole situation felt like something that would play out on a sitcom like Seinfeld. I realized after a few minutes that I was going to end up talking the entire session. So, instead of being annoyed and disappointed, I pretended I was actually on a sitcom. I was the character who had specific expectations who ended up having them all dashed by a character who was juxtaposed to their role. My relaxation massage was being delivered by a high energy social butterfly and just for fun, she was foreign.

At this point, I could easily believe that we could coincidentally share so many things in common. But then...

"What do you do for fun?" She asked.

"I write songs," I replied, trying to find something we didn't have in common.

She gasped. "Me, too!"

"I play the piano."

"Me too. I play piano."

"And I sing."

"Yes, I sing too. I am writing a song that goes..." she proceeded to sing in a foreign language and with a melody I couldn't seem to make out the chord progression for. After a verse, I'm guessing, she stopped and sighed. I could hear the smile in her sigh. "Do you like it? It's a very pretty song."

"Very. I also like to write movies," I said.

"You know, I started writing a movie, too."

She spoke with total sincerity. I didn't know what to believe. Maybe it was true, maybe it wasn't. Maybe she really did also get divorced the same year I did and maybe she really doesn't eat pork. And maybe she did play ten different instruments when she was a teenager. Maybe.

In movies, some of the best characters drive everyone around them crazy. My advice is that if you have to interact with an annoying or extreme person, cast them into your life and learn to find them entertaining. But when you do this, enjoy them with sincerity and without judgment. I don't look down on that woman who claimed to have everything in common with me. It was an odd experience, but I enjoyed her for who she was.

I also enjoy ornery people. They can be really tough to work with, but they can also be hilarious without trying. Extreme characters will always present a challenge to those around them, but they will also create opportunities to create memories. People who push our buttons will become lasting memories (because they increase our level of emotions, which triggers our brains to create memories). Why not find a way to enjoy them on some level?

And if YOU are that wonderfully weird character, embrace it. Of course, it's important to continue to mature in social intelligence and sensitivity, but don't stifle who you are. I've always had a reputation of being weird, wacky, even annoying, but it's all that "differentness" that allows me to do what I do. I do my best to bring people more joy than pain.

I don't always get it right, some people don't like me no matter what I try, and sometimes I overwhelm people. If I were to be completely vulnerable, I'd say that there've been times when I've feared that people will tire of me and reject me, so I've behaved with a heightened sense of awareness in order to assess moment by moment who I need to be; what to say, what to do in order to make people like me. But masking is exhausting and unfruitful in the long run. Your Author made you in a very unique way. He loves diversity. Just look at how many types of animals and plants there are. The one who created the majestic Bengal tiger also created the red-lipped batfish.

Your true friends won't just toss you aside because you're different or odd. You'll be able to relax with them. Maybe not all your jokes will land how you want them to, but they'll love you so they won't hold that against you. Maybe it's more work to be friends with you, but to them, you're worth the work.

My friends in Mexico are incredibly patient with me while I speak broken Spanish. They regularly have to wait while I look up a word, but they don't grow impatient with me. They love to help teach me new words and phrases. They have a good laugh at some of my strange ways of speaking, or my innocent mistakes, like when I accidentally got "maquillaje" (make-up) and "mantequilla" (butter) mixed up. I said I needed to buy more mantequilla for my face. It's now a running joke. They're not looking down on me when they're laughing, they're just enjoying me. And one day, I'm going to be fluent and they'll have been an important part of my journey to get there.

Find what makes you unique and capitalize on it. It was placed in you for a reason. One time, I had a job working for a litigation lawyer. Oh my goodness, I nearly died of boredom and I was incredibly grateful when I was fired. My boss and I liked each other as people, but I was so far out of my element that I was practically useless. But give me a mic and a stage and I'll shine. Most people fear public speaking. I don't even need to prepare. (I do prepare, though. For those who want to hire me to come speak, I promise, I will arrive prepared and professional. I'm just saying I don't turn down a stage even if someone springs it on me.) I can entertain to fill time like nobody's business!

That's what I want for you. I want you to find your element so you can shine. It'll be strongly connected to what makes you specifically you. That unique combination of attributes that your Author wrote into your character will help you to find the people, job, and activities that will bring out more of your character.

I get it, though. It's not easy to pursue who you really are because it demands vulnerability. In a way, we're exposed as we reveal our true selves to the world. If we mask and pretend to be someone we're not, then when people judge us, they're not really judging us; they're judging the person we're pretending to be. That hurts a lot less. But to spend your whole life pretending... We get one shot at this. We don't get to come back and do it with courage the next time. This is it. (Yes, I did just more or less say "you only live once". YOLO!) The need for courage is part of the human experience. We're all faced with times in which we need to press into courage in order to progress.

The coolest thing is when we find people that totally get us. I once had this roommate who completely understood my sense of humor. The little things like subtle pauses as I refrained from saying something (she totally knew what I wasn't saying) to the things I blurted out before I realized it might not be the most sensitive thing to say. For example, her mother had passed away the same week she moved in with me and over the following weeks and months, she sorted through all of her mother's belongings in our storage room. It was a difficult time, obviously, so sometimes, I'd keep her company. One time, she was staring at a blanket that her mother had really liked. For some reason, she felt obligated to keep it even though she really didn't want it. She asked me what she should do.

"Are you going to use it?" I asked her.

"No… I really don't want to keep it, but…"

"So, get rid of it. She'll never know."

She stared at me, the blanket in her hands, and then burst into laughter. It was only then that I realized the extent of what I'd said and I was beyond grateful that she laughed and didn't cry or kick me out.

She lived with me and my young boys for a year. During that time, we ended up having a million inside jokes and amazing conversations. One time, we were getting the table ready for dinner. My father was visiting and my kids were running around. I don't remember all of what the conversation was about, but I do recall that we had so many inside jokes that she and I were in stitches of laughter and my dad was just staring at us, confused.

At one point he actually said, "I don't get it, did I miss something? Why is she laughing?"

"Because I'm funny," I replied with a shrug.

He glanced between us, totally deadpan. "Huh."

"Yep." I replied, mirroring his level of emotion.

44

Which, of course, sent her reeling, and me soon after.

The funny thing is that we didn't actually know each other very well when she moved in. We had only met once or twice before with a mutual friend. But we clicked immediately. My dad didn't pick up on the subtleties of my humor, but she did.

And that brings me to my final point of the chapter. While it's awesome when you can find people you click with, there will also be people who don't totally get you, but they love you regardless. Sometimes, my parents get my jokes. Other times, they miss them completely. But they're still my biggest fans. They saw my potential for music when I was five years old and put me into lessons. They even went as far as to force me to practice because they didn't want me to miss out on my own capacity because I was rebellious, impulsive and strong-willed. (I didn't like to play what was assigned, I much preferred to play my own songs my own way. I even arranged my own cover versions of classical songs. I don't know why my teacher wasn't impressed by that.)

Like all parents, mine didn't have a clear vision of my future. But they did recognize my unique traits and did their best to foster maturity in those areas. They supported opportunities for me to be on stage, but they also taught me to accept that I needed to share attention in the room and not be a hog. They taught me to pursue being the best, but to remember there is always going to be someone who is better. Humility is not an easy trait to teach a born performer without stifling their joy. They did what they could to teach me and life took care of the rest.

Psalm 139 expresses God's care in creating your body. But your Author also put a lot of thought into creating the attributes that contribute to your personality. He gave you a combination unlike anyone else. No matter the social pressures, you don't need to be like your neighbor. That character's already been assigned to someone else. You need to be you because if you don't, the world will never get to know that beautifully unique character that our Author lovingly wrote.

Chapter 5
Good News, Bad News

Welcome to life. There's good news and bad news.

Everything changes. Nothing stays the same. Depending on what season you're currently in, the statement, "This, too, shall pass," will either give you a sense of relief or sorrow. Of course we always want the good moments to last forever, but that's just not how it works.

Therefore, cherish what you have while you have it. You might have the thought that it's just the calm before the storm, but even if that's true, enjoy it without the anxiety of impending doom. Seasons come and go and come back around. That's guaranteed. But, the strange thing is we so often fight it. My characters fight it. Mostly because they don't know what season they're supposed to be in. They just know they're not where they used to be and they don't like it. But "change" is more than just inevitable, it's what drives the story forward.

Believe it or not, that was the good news. The bad news is that conflict also moves the story forward.

If we have too long in the story without conflict, it starts to drag and become repetitive. Conflict is a necessary path for progression as it wakes people up and gets them to make decisions. But not just conflict for the sake of conflict. Contrived conflict is poor writing, and super immature - don't do it. Authentic conflict, where the characters have legitimate differences that cause friction, allows for the deeper story to eventually come out.

As I mentioned in Chapter 2, I'll put my hero in all kinds of difficult situations. But let me be clear, I never put my character in such horrible circumstances without purpose. In fact, I never do anything that lacks purpose within the story. I can't afford to waste space on the page for meaningless things. I've got one and a half to two hours to introduce a compelling character, create context, take the character on a meaningful and entertaining journey, to a meaningful and entertaining conclusion. And most of the time, I also want it to be inspiring and empowering for my audience.

I've learned not to avoid conflict, but to embrace its purpose; to mine deeper into the person I'm created to be. I'm not saying that conflict has become easy. It's still incredibly difficult and stressful. But the growth that comes afterward is more valuable than my fear is powerful. This is, in essence, what my characters learn as well. That piece of themselves that they were either avoiding or unaware of can only be realized by mustering up the courage to face the conflict head-on. At the end of a movie, the hero has a tete-a-tete with their adversary. This could be a moment where they annihilate their enemy, but it could also be as simple as looking them in the eye, unintimidated. They're over it, whatever "it" was. That's what's on the other side of purposeful conflict. Peace. Confidence. Courage.

If you're someone who fears conflict, welcome to the club. If you're ready for victory, now you know what you have to do. I know that may sound over simplified, but it's the truth. And just because something is simple, doesn't mean it's easy. If you're anything like the characters in my movies, you're probably thinking, "Yeah, but I'm not like that, I can't... it's just not in me." And to that, I will discreetly hide the smile on my face. The reality is that you don't actually know what you're capable of until you've done it.

"Words" is a short script I wrote that shows the internal journey of a man as he processes difficult memories. I'm including the entire script here so you can see the full story and journey, instead of just specific parts. What I want you to notice is where he starts. And then see where he's at in the end.

EXT. GRAVEYARD - DAY

BILL, 64, sits in his truck and stares out the window at a gravesite. The weight of the world is on his shoulders.

                    BILL (V.O.)
          I can still remember loving him...
          which makes hating him so complicated.

BEGIN FLASHBACK

EXT. BILL'S CHILDHOOD HOME - DAY 1950'S

BILLY, Bill at age 6, sits on the porch, near MICHAEL, 30, Billy's father, who sits on a chair, both whittling. The sun shines brightly on this nostalgic image.

Michael smiles and winks at Billy, then takes a swig of beer.

                    BILL (V.O.)
          When he smiled at me, I could conquer
          the world.

Billy smiles adoringly at Michael.

Michael invites him to sit on his lap and he gladly accepts.

                    BILL (V.O.)
          I wanted to be just like him. Or at
          least...

Fade to black.

                    BILL (V.O.)
          I wanted to be like who he was in the
          daytime.

INT. BILL'S CHILDHOOD HOME - NIGHT

Billy, fearfully runs through the hallway. Michael
chases after him in a drunken rage with a mostly
empty half-gallon bottle of whiskey gripped in his
hand.

                    BILL (V.O.)
          I wish I'd gone to bed early that
          night. Maybe things would've been
          different between us.

Michael catches Billy and sits on top of him. WENDY,
24, Michael's pregnant wife, frantically tries to
pull Michael off of Billy.

                    BILL (V.O.)
          Maybe.

Michael takes a swig, eyes burning into Billy as he
projects his own self-loathing onto his son.

He raises his hand, ready to knock Billy into next
week. Billy covers his face with his arms to block
the blow.

Cut to black.

END FLASHBACK

EXT. GRAVEYARD - DAY

Bill slowly gets out of the truck and closes the
door. He begrudgingly walks toward the grave he was
staring at.

Bill stops at the grave and stares at the epitaph
which reads "MICHAEL UNGER"

BEGIN FLASHBACK

INT. HOSPITAL - NIGHT

Billy lays in the hospital bed, unconscious, bruised
and swollen. Wendy and Michael stand next to the bed,
talking with the DOCTOR.

The Doctor nervously glances over at the door and TWO
POLICE OFFICERS, a SOCIAL WORKER, and two SECURITY
GUARDS enter.

Wendy panics hysterically while Michael is forced
into handcuffs and escorted out.

The Social Worker steps over to Billy and glares at
Wendy.

                    BILL (V.O.)
          A kid can only be so clumsy before
          someone figures it out.

Wendy's panic increases.

INT. BILLY'S FOSTER HOME - DAY

Billy, covered in bruises, arm in a sling, cautiously
follows a FOSTER PARENT into a dump of a house.

The foster parent shows him his room, a tiny room
with a stained mattress on the floor, mangled blinds,
and a hole in the wall.

Billy enters, sits on the bed and stares blankly.

                    BILL (V.O.)
          I stopped talking after that.

INT. BILL'S CHILDHOOD HOME - DAY 1960'S

BILLY, now 12, sits on the front porch, whittling,
while his younger sister RENEE, 5, plays with a doll
nearby.

A car drives into the driveway. Renee jumps up and
runs to the car. Billy stands at the edge of the
porch, watching with mixed emotions.

                    RENEE
          Daddy!

Michael exits the car and Renee jumps into his arms.

                    MICHAEL
          Come here, baby girl. You're gettin'
          so big.

Wendy exits the car with a huge smile. Everyone makes
their way toward the house.

                    MICHAEL (CONT'D)
                 (off Billy)
          What you got there, boy?

Billy hides the wood that's been mostly whittled into
a dog.

                    MICHAEL (CONT'D)
          C'mon now, let me see.

Billy reluctantly hands it to Michael to inspect.

                    MICHAEL (CONT'D)
          You did this?

Billy nods.

Michael looks at Wendy who shoots him a "be kind" look.

                    MICHAEL (CONT'D)
          It's uh... it's pretty good. A horse,
          right?

                         RENEE
          No, Daddy, it's a dog.

                        MICHAEL
          Oh... well, maybe your next dog will
          look less like a horse, huh?

Billy nods, takes the dog back and runs inside.

                    MICHAEL (CONT'D)
               (off Wendy)
          He talking yet?

Wendy shakes her head.

                         WENDY
          (off Renee)
          Go on inside, honey. We'll be in
          shortly.

Renee enters the house.

Michael sits on the porch chair. Wendy sits on his lap.

                    WENDY (CONT'D)
          He's coming around, Michael --

                        MICHAEL
          It's not right. He's twelve. I should
          be able to have a conversation with my
          own son.

                              WENDY
          I know. Just give it time.

                             MICHAEL
          It's been over five years! How much
          time d --

The front door opens and Billy steps onto the porch,
carrying an armload of whittled creations.

                              WENDY
          What's that, baby?

                             MICHAEL
          He's not a baby, Wendy.
                    (off Billy)
          He's a man... right?

Billy reveals a shy smile and steps toward Michael.
Wendy stands to make room.

Billy hands Michael an eagle. Michael raises his
eyebrows.

                      MICHAEL (CONT'D)
          What's this one?

                              WENDY
          It's a--

                             MICHAEL
                    (off Wendy)
          No! I want him to tell me.
                    (off Billy)
          What is it?

Billy looks to Wendy for help. Michael turns Billy's
face to look him in the eye.

                               54

                    MICHAEL (CONT'D)
No... look at me. You can do this.
Billy's breathing increases, growing
anxious.

                    MICHAEL (CONT'D)
                  (forcing patience)
What's it called?

Billy reaches to take it back, Michael evades the
snatch.

                    MICHAEL (CONT'D)
I know you can talk! Just say it!

                    WENDY
Michael!

                    MICHAEL
          (off Billy)
Come on! Say it!

Billy's eyes well up and he runs back into the house.

                    WENDY
                  (carefully)
Michael, you can't just--

                    MICHAEL
He's my son! Stay out of it!

Wendy reluctantly bites her tongue.

INT. BILLY'S BEDROOM - DAY

Billy methodically lines his whittled creations up
along his windowsill. Michael, passing by, notices
and stops.

                    MICHAEL
What knife do you use?

55

Billy, startled, turns around. Michael raises his
hands to show he comes in peace.

                    MICHAEL (CONT'D)
               It's just me, boy.

Billy hands the jack-knife from his dresser to
Michael. Michael inspects it and raises his eyebrows.

                    MICHAEL (CONT'D)
               It's a nice one... where'd you get it?

Billy points out of his room, referring to Wendy.

                    MICHAEL (CONT'D)
               C'mon, now... speak up. I don't
               understand your hand signals.

Billy swallows hard. He looks at the door like he
wants to bolt, but Michael's in the way.

                    MICHAEL (CONT'D)
               She ain't home.

Billy stares, horrified.

                    MICHAEL (CONT'D)
               One word, Billy. And I'll leave you
               be.

Billy starts to hyperventilate.

                    WENDY (O.S.)
               Michael, Billy... we're home. Can you
               come help with the groceries, please?

Michael stares a moment at Billy.

                    MICHAEL
               Well, go on, then.

                         56

Billy runs out of the room. Michael casually follows.

INT. KITCHEN - EVENING

The family sits around the table for dinner. Billy
reaches for the salt. Michael snatches it and holds
it up.

                    MICHAEL
          (off Billy)
     Ask me for it.

                    WENDY
     Michael, please...

                    MICHAEL
          (off Wendy)
     Stay out of it.

Wendy bites her tongue and watches nervously. Michael
gets in Billy's face.

                    MICHAEL (CONT'D)
     Say it... Salt.

Billy stares at his plate, his breathing growing
heavier.

                    MICHAEL (CONT'D)
     That game may have worked on your
     mama, but it won't work on me! Say it!

Renee watches in confused fear. Wendy grabs Michael's
arm.

                    WENDY
     Michael--

Michael shoves Wendy's hold off him.

                    MICHAEL
          I said stay out of it!

Renee starts to cry.

                    MICHAEL (CONT'D)
          Shut her up!

                    WENDY
          Michael, let's just eat --

Michael stands in frustration and towers over Billy.

                    MICHAEL
          Say it, Billy! Salt! Say it!

                    WENDY
          You're scaring Renee!

                    MICHAEL
          Then he better start talking!

Wendy sees Michael make a fist. She stands and pulls
on his arm.

                    WENDY
          Michael! He's had enough!

Michael shoves Wendy up against the wall.

                    MICHAEL
          I'll say when it's enough!

                    WENDY
          He's just a kid!

Michael backhands Wendy, throwing her to the floor.

                    BILLY (O.S.)
                  (forced)
          S-salt!

                         58

Michael and Wendy turn to Billy, amazed. Billy stands, stiff as a board, mind racing. Michael slowly moves toward Billy.

                    MICHAEL
          See, I knew you could...

Billy runs out of the house.

                    MICHAEL (CONT'D)
          Billy!

Michael chases after him.

                    MICHAEL (CONT'D)
          Billy!

EXT. BILL'S CHILDHOOD HOME - CONTINUOUS

Billy races down the front steps toward the street.

Michael catches Billy in the front yard and they stumble to the ground.

Billy, face down, fights with all his might to break free.

Michael, on his knees hovering over Billy, turns Billy over to face him.

                    MICHAEL
          Whoa! Settle down!

Michael catches a fist in his face.

                    MICHAEL (CONT'D)
          Hey!

Michael slaps Billy in the face. Billy freezes and closes his eyes. Michael silently scolds himself.

                    MICHAEL (CONT'D)
          Look, I'm -- I didn't mean it. You
          just got me good and I reacted.

Billy doesn't move.

                    MICHAEL (CONT'D)
          Now, don't start this again.

                    BILLY
               (under his breath)
          I w-wish you'd never come home.

                    MICHAEL
               (intrigued)
          What was that? What'd you say?

Billy opens his eyes and glares at Michael.

                    BILLY
          I... I wish you'd never c-come home! I
          wish they w-would've kept you locked-
          up f-f-forever!

Michael stares at Billy, a combination of proud and
hurt. Billy glares at his father and then shuts his
eyes tight. Michael looks around, processing.

Wendy looks on, scared.

Michael swallows and slowly stands.

Billy stays on the ground, eyes squeezed shut, full
of fear and breathing heavily.

                    WENDY (O.S.)
          Michael? Michael, where are you going?

Off screen, the car door OPENS and SLAMS SHUT. Billy
stays frozen, eyes clenched, BREATHING HEAVILY.

                          60

                    WENDY (O.S.) (CONT'D)
          Michael!

Off screen, the car STARTS and PEELS OUT of the
driveway and takes off down the road.

                    WENDY (O.S.) (CONT'D)
          Michael!

Billy slowly opens his eyes to see his mother
standing at the end of the driveway, watching Michael
turn the corner at the end of the street.

Billy's emotions reflect a combination of sadness and
relief.

END FLASHBACK

EXT. GRAVEYARD - DAY

Bill stands at the gravesite, with the same
combination of emotions on his face.

His eyes shift as he recalls another memory.

                    BILL (V.O.)
          That was the last time I saw him...

BEGIN FLASHBACK

EXT. GROCERY STORE - DAY 1980'S

Bill, now 28, exits a grocery store holding a paper
bag of groceries in one arm and his 4-year-old
daughter, AMELIA's hand in the other. Amelia skips
along in a pleasant bliss.

                    BILL (V.O.)
          ... Until the very last time I saw
          him.

Bill smiles at his daughter, then looks out ahead, glancing around as they approach the parking lot.

Michael, now 50's, smokes a cigarette as he approaches the store. At first, he doesn't see Bill.

> BILL (V.O.)
> I didn't know if he'd even recognize
> me.

Bill stands frozen at the edge of the curb.

Michael recognizes Bill and pauses momentarily before continuing to bring his cigarette to his mouth and look away.

> BILL (V.O.)
> I had both dreaded and wished for that
> moment for twenty years.

Michael passes Bill without a word, though they see each other, clearly aware, and enters the store.

> AMELIA (O.S.)
> Daddy... Daddy...

Amelia pulls on her father's hand.

> AMELIA (CONT'D)
> Who's that, Daddy?

> BILL
> It's my... uh... just... someone I
> used to know.

> AMELIA
> Aren't ya gonna say hi?

Bill holds back his tears.

                          BILL
           C'mon, let's go.

Bill walks with Amelia through the parking lot.

INT. SHOWER - NIGHT

28-year-old Bill stands in the shower, leaning
against the wall, sobbing like the weight of his
heart is crushing him.

END FLASHBACK

EXT. GRAVEYARD - DAY

Bill stands at the gravesite, staring at the ground.

BEGIN FLASHBACK

EXT. BILL'S CHILDHOOD HOME - DAY 1950'S

Michael swings 6-year-old Billy around and playfully
wrestles with him, both laughing, fades in and out to
black.

                       BILL (V.O.)
            A part of me will always love him and
            miss him.

EXT. BILL'S CHILDHOOD HOME - DAY 1960'S

A brief memory of Michael chasing a fearful 12-year-
old Billy through the yard fades in and out to black.

                       BILL (V.O.)
            A part of me will always fear him.

EXT. GROCERY STORE - DAY 1980'S

A brief memory of Bill standing frozen at the curb as Michael approaches to pass by him, fades in and out to black.

                    BILL (V.O.)
          A part of me will always wonder if he
          ever loved me.

END FLASHBACK

EXT. GRAVEYARD - DAY

64-year-old Bill stands at the gravesite.

He looks up to see a 36-year-old version of his father, standing behind the epitaph with 28-year-old Bill, 12-year-old Billy, and 6-year-old Billy standing just behind him.

                    BILL
          You can't have them.

Michael stares at Bill, emotionless. The younger Bills remain silent where they are as if trapped.

                    BILL (CONT'D)
          You can't have them! They belong to
          me!

He buckles to his knees, sobbing.

                    BILL (V.O.)
          We think when we age that we become
          something new; that the one-year-old
          is replaced by a two-year-old. Two by
          three, and so on. But the truth is
          that we just acquire them.

The younger versions of Bill watch him with a desire to help him but are unable to.

                    BILL (V.O.)
I'm not just sixty-four. I'm also
twenty-eight, twelve, and six... and
everything in between. And we all
needed one thing. But only I could
make it happen.

Bill regains a semblance of composure and stands with
renewed strength and dignity.

                    BILL
          (off Michael)
     I forgive you.

28-year-old Bill now stands on 64-year-old Bill's
side.

                    BILL (CONT'D)
          (off Michael)
     I forgive you.

12-year-old Billy now stands on 64-year-old Bill's
side.

He looks at the bruised and beaten 6-year-old Billy
standing alone behind Michael.

                    BILL (CONT'D)
          (off Michael, with great
          effort)
     I forgive you.

6-year-old Billy now stands with the group of Bills.

64-year-old Bill stares at Michael as the weight of
the world gradually lifts off of him.

                    BILL (CONT'D)
          (calm, resolved)
     Good-bye.

64-year-old Bill turns to walk back to his truck.

28-year-old Bill looks Michael in the eye then turns and follows Bill.

12-year-old Billy does the same. Michael watches, powerless.

6-year-old Billy without bruises, stares at his father for a few moments. A slight smile brightens Billy's face before he runs to catch up to the other Bills.

The four Bills approach the truck.

64-year-old Bill climbs in and looks back where he came from. Michael and the other Bills are gone.

Bill stares a moment, then nods with peaceful resolve and starts the truck.

Like many people, Bill's relationship with his "enemy" is complicated. Not only because it's his own father, but because it gets inside his own head. Even after his father dies, Bill still carries the pain and trauma of the past. Choosing to embrace the conflict with your adversary head-on is never easy. Every single one of my characters has no idea what they're capable of at the start of their story.

Whatever, "I can't" statement you've let yourself believe, I challenge you to ask the question, "Says who?" Who says you can't? Who says you can't get healthy? Who says you can't set and enforce boundaries? Who says you can't get into university? Whatever your "I can't" statement is, my question is, "Says who?" The only one who has the right to tell you, you can't, is your Author, yet he's the one telling you that you can.

If you discover that your Author is leading you on a journey toward something that feels impossible, what are you going to do with that? Keep in mind that your Author is going to be more invested in getting you to the goal than you are in avoiding it. If your Author is setting you on a journey and challenging you to grow, it's because you CAN. In fact, the reality that you're capable of so much more than you can currently imagine is astounding.

So many of my characters couldn't even fathom at the start of the story that they could ever end up where they did. Watch your favorite movies and tell me that's not the truth. Watch it and let it resonate within you. It's okay if you can't see your future. Your Author can and he's already there with you.

Chapter 6
Miracles

Ever wonder how many miracles have happened in your life that, because they happened, you had no clue they happened?

A miracle is the only time I get to interject myself into a story. It's the only time I get to control circumstances solely because it's my right and ability to do so. Typically, as writers, we have a rule; one miracle (or major coincidence) per story.

Thankfully, God isn't bound to North American screenwriting rules. Miracles are His jam. That's why the only movies with several miracles are ones that are based on a true story. If it didn't actually happen in real life, no one would believe it. And even at that, there are several movies that couldn't include all the miracles that took place in a situation because it would overwhelm the story. God is good, my friend. But let's get honest about miracles from the perspective of the human experience.

Many believers in Almighty God also believe that He's able to perform miracles. The Bible has several examples of God interjecting himself into his story via miracles. And how do his people respond to receiving the miracle? Well, it's a bit of a mixed bag. Some people lose their faith before the miracle happens. Some people take it for granted. But others receive it with awe and gratitude.

Our emotional maturity plays a huge part in how we perceive life, including spiritual situations. Many people who wish they could witness a miracle are completely unaware of what they're asking for. In order to witness a miracle, God making a way where there is no way, the situation has to become impossible. What do you do when you're in an impossible situation? Do you lose your faith? Complain? Turn bitter? Believe it or not, our heart just before we receive the miracle is more important than how we respond to it.

When I was a single parent and barely making ends meet, I, at one point, had only enough for that particular month. If I was careful, I'd be able to keep my boys and I fed throughout that month. But I had no money lined up to be able to pay rent when the next month came. I had been praying and trusting God, but this was getting pretty scary for me. I didn't know what I'd do if I got kicked out of my apartment.

As I prayed about my situation, I felt God calling my attention. First, a reflection caught my eye and I turned around to see the most incredible sunset I've ever seen in my life. As I marveled at it, I heard God say in my spirit, "That's how much I love you." It stunned me. It also stumped me. I stared at the incredible artwork in the sky, dumbfounded as to what I had just heard God say. I didn't dare ask what it meant yet. I knew it was important and that I needed to capture every detail of the moment.

Next, I felt my attention drawn to a field of blueberries. "That's how much I love you." Then, it was a snow-capped mountain. "That's how much I love you." It overwhelmed me. I knew it carried great significance, not just because he was taking the time to speak to me specifically, but because he was repeating it. I had an understanding that I could look at literally every aspect of creation and know he was saying the same thing in response to it. I cherished it in my heart and did my utmost to figure out what it meant. He wasn't just saying that he loved me. He wanted me to understand the depth of it. But, I didn't get it.

The next day, I humbly approached God in prayer and confessed that I didn't understand the message. I prayed, "God, I thank you for speaking to me, but I'm confused. What do you mean when you say, 'That's how much I love you'? Do you mean your love is as beautiful as the sunset? As sweet as the fruit? As high as a mountain? What does it mean?"

Gently, but as if it was supposed to be obvious, he responded, "Can you paint the sunset in the sky? Can you bring forth fruit in its season? Can you raise up a mountain?"

"No," I responded, still not getting it.

"That's how much I love you. I love you in ways you cannot love yourself. I love your boys in ways you can't love them. I got this."

I had this incredible sense of compassion from him that he understood the source of my anxiety. But it also felt like it was mixed with the confidence of an expert who's holding back a smile because he knows he's so good at what he does that my anxiety is adorably misplaced. I received and embraced the message and went on with my life.

A couple of weeks later, just a few days before the end of the month, I was literally in no better position, financially. Anxiety was working its way back into my gut. I decided to read the psalms because I needed to encourage myself in the Lord.

As I opened my Bible and began flipping to the book of Psalms, I passed by the book of Job and remembered that God spoke directly to Job. I wanted to hear directly from God, too. I was starting to doubt my conversation with Him, and I wondered if I'd imagined it. I knew I didn't, but doubt can make you question even a miracle. I chose to read the words God spoke to Job instead. Segments from the book of

Job, chapters 38-41. (I encourage you to read the entirety of the chapters as God took a lot of time to speak with Job directly.)

Then the Lord spoke to Job out of the storm. He said, "Who is this that obscures my plans with words without knowledge? Brace yourself like a man; I will question you, and you shall answer me.

Where were you when I laid the earth's foundation? Tell me, if you understand. Who marked off its dimensions? Surely you know! Who stretched a measuring line across it? On what were its footings set, or who laid its cornerstone while the morning stars sang together and all the angels shouted for joy?

"Have you ever given orders to the morning, or shown the dawn its place, that it might take the earth by the edges and shake the wicked out of it?

"Have you journeyed to the springs of the sea or walked in the recesses of the deep? Have the gates of death been shown to you? Have you seen the gates of the deepest darkness? Have you comprehended the vast expanses of the earth? Tell me, if you know all this.

"Can you bind the chains of the Pleiades? Can you loosen Orion's belt? Can you bring forth the constellations in their seasons or lead out the Bear with its cubs? Do you know the laws of the heavens? Can you set up God's dominion over the earth?

"Do you give the horse its strength or clothe its neck with a flowing mane? Do you make it leap like a locust, striking terror with its proud snorting? Will the one who contends with the Almighty correct him? Let him who accuses God answer him!"

Then Job answered the Lord:

"I am unworthy. How can I reply to you? I put my hand over my mouth. I spoke once, but I have no answer. Twice, but I will say no more."

After reading the entire conversation between God and Job, I set my Bible down and stared into space in absolute awe. I'd always read this portion of scripture as a rebuke. But there it was; pretty much the same conversation I'd had with God just a couple of weeks previous. And maybe it was a rebuke. Maybe God had given me a rebuke, but it was so wrapped in love that it calmed my fear and anxiety. It was the most beautiful rebuke I could've ever received. What an incredible Creator. No wonder Job had nothing to say in response other than to admit that God was God and Job was not and to repent for suggesting God owed him anything.

I immediately prayed and repented for doubting the conversation with God. I thanked him for his grace and love and renewed my resolve to trust that God had a plan.

On the very last day of the month, my bank account had $1800 deposited into it, which was enough to cover two months worth of rent. It turns out that some financial aid I'd applied for had been approved and backdated. I wasn't expecting to hear from them for at least another month and there was no guarantee that I would even be approved. I had received my miracle.

But what I realized was that the true miracle was what transpired in the weeks before the money ended up in my bank account. I had conversed with the Holy Spirit. I learned to trust that God could make a way when there appeared to be no way. I grasped the fact that God's love and concern for me and my children is vast and beyond comprehension. I rested in his assurance before I had proof.

Experiencing a miracle is amazing. It gives you an incredible testimony and touch point in your life to call back on. After God led the Israelites out of Egypt, he instructed them to celebrate a yearly memorial of the event to recall his goodness and authority.

Passover continues to be celebrated to this day. But when you read the account of it, you'll see that there were several people who grumbled that God saved them from one horrible situation only to create another. They had no faith that if God could deliver them from Egypt that he could also take care of them in the desert. It's easy to look back on them in judgment, but let's take a look at the reality of the human experience.

I think that since experiencing a miracle feels like such a rare event, we assume we only get one, if any. If we've already experienced one miracle, we're doomed when the next shoe drops. But what I've learned is that the "just one miracle" rule only applies to screenwriting. In real life, when we invite God into our lives, we get to interact with him on a regular basis.

Just like in the book of Exodus, after God revealed his power through the 10 plagues, then led the Israelites out into the desert, he had a plan for the next step of the way. He wanted to give them such a strong taste of his goodness and provision that they would never doubt again. I've seen it in my own life.

After that miracle of money showing up just when I needed it, I totally relaxed. I recall a few months later, someone asked me why I wasn't worried about the next month to come. I replied, "God knows that November comes after October. He's not shortsighted like that." My responsibility was to obey and to be a good steward of my resources. During that season of my life, my Author wanted it to be completely clear to me that HE was sustaining me.

During that season, I not only struggled to find permanent employment, but I also needed clothes that fit. As I matured in my walk with the Lord, I realized that I had some clothing that lacked modesty. I also had several garments that had worn out.

One day, I stood in front of my closet and drawers and prayed for provision. I heard in my spirit, "Make room." So, I pulled out everything that was worn or did not honor God. Two days later, the mother of a student in my son's kindergarten class sheepishly asked if I was interested in her hand-me-downs. I was amazed! They turned out to fit me perfectly and they were classy outfits. I was able to feel confident in my clothes again.

During this same season of life, I ended up with a bad case of vertigo. It's the only time I've ever had it in my life. I don't know what caused it, but I will say that God used it to show me He had my back. My cousin picked my boys up in the morning and took them to school. And the new friend who gave me the clothes dropped the kids off after school. Since I had recently moved to a new city, I started attending a new church. As part of the church's follow-up for newcomers, one of the pastors sent me an email to check-in on their new attendee. I wrote back that I was actually flat on my back in bed with vertigo. Within a few hours, some women showed up at my door with casseroles. I couldn't move without vomiting for about three days, and it took at least another week or more before I was able to drive again, but during that time, my household didn't miss a beat.

My kids went to school, we had meals to eat, my children stepped up to avoid fighting and do all the stuff they needed to do, like bathe, brush their teeth, and go to bed on time. (I found this incredibly encouraging because, as a single mother, I often questioned if I was doing right by them. In this situation, I saw their compassion for me and desire to be helpful and obedient shine through.) Someone even helped to clean my house and do laundry. It was very humbling, but it also revealed to me that God could lay my needs on people's hearts and take care of me. Every single person who helped during that time was a Christian. I couldn't help but think about Jesus' words in John

13:35 "This is how they will know you are my disciples; by your love for one another."

One miracle after another proved to me that God is very much in control. And then, I started to realize that in order for me to see that, he had to let things get desperate. I came to realize also that He doesn't enjoy seeing us in times of desperation and therefore he often intervenes before we even realize the potential of desperation is on the horizon. We take for granted the lack of witnessing a miracle. God is happy to care for us because he loves us. And oftentimes, he'll do it in secret. He even does it while we pray for the opposite. How many times has God kept a door closed, frustrating us, only to realize in hindsight that God saved us from our own ignorance?

If you have not yet experienced seeing the hand of God move, I encourage you to seek out an adventure with God. Set one day (or even half a day) aside per week for a month. During that time, ask God what he wants to do. Be prepared to provide an act of service, share your resources, or talk to people. More than likely, God will call you out of your comfort zone. And if you haven't learned to discern the voice of God calling you yet, or if you don't hear something specific, then choose something that the Bible states matters to God. (Don't just sit in prayer, waiting. Get up and do something.) Providing for widows, orphans, homeless, disabled, imprisoned, and lonely people, is a great place to start.

As you care about the things that our loving Creator cares about, your spirit will mature and you'll witness Him move. At the end of the month, you just might want to continue. Regardless of how you organize your time, the fact is that when you make yourself available to God, he won't pass that up. You might be the answer to someone else's desperation. God might partner with you to provide a miracle.

Chapter 7
Perspective

Perspective is everything. And everyone has one. But not the same one.

Have you ever stopped to think about that movie you really enjoyed? The one with all of those really compelling characters that seemed to all be so individual and unique. Those were all written by the same person (or group of people).

In my screenplays, I'm the one that writes the hero, the villain, the mentor, the child, the foreigner, the mentally ill, etc... How do I give them all their own ideas and personalities so they can be distinct individuals? As I mentioned in a previous chapter, I gift each of my characters with attributes, skills, talents, wounds, a historical framework through which they see the world (a backstory), dreams, fears, passions, and flaws. Since each character is given a unique combination of these things, they end up with distinct personalities and worldviews, i.e., I give them each their own perspective.

Before we dive into perspective, let's have some fun with an opening scene from one of my comedies.

Opening scene from The Three Amigas, written by
Jaclyn Whitt:

INT. AIRPLANE - DAY

PASSENGERS board the plane.

VICTORIA, 46, a divorced control-freak and devoted
mother, carries carry-on luggage for herself and her
daughter, LIV, 17, a high-strung girl with zero
social appropriateness filters.

Liv has an emotional meltdown while Victoria scoots
her forward, little by little.

                    LIV
          I can't do this. Mom, I can't. Tina
          will understand.

                    VICTORIA
          You're going to your sister's wedding.

                    LIV
          Mom, I'm serious. I. Don't. Do.
          Planes!

                    VICTORIA
          Liv, it's just a two-hour flight.

                    LIV
          Two hours? Two whole hou-- Mom! I
          can't even handle two minutes. Look at
          me. We're not even off the ground and
          I'm--

                    VICTORIA
          Breathe, Liv. In, two, three, out,
          two, three. In, two, three...

Liv follows the breathing counting, then gives up.

78

                         LIV
        It's not working!

                       VICTORIA
        Because you have to do it longer!

Passengers around stare at Victoria's outburst.

Victoria calms herself, offering an apologetic smile.

Liv collapses onto the seat.

                       VICTORIA
        Just... keep breathing.

                         LIV
        Spinning... in all directions.

Victoria loads the carry-ons into the overhead
compartment.

                       VICTORIA
        Liv, I've flown countless times. If
        there's anything to worry about dying
        from, it's boredom!

CUT TO:

INT. AIRPLANE - LATER

Panic ensues on the jolting plane as it passes
through severe turbulence.

Luggage explodes out of overhead compartments.

Passengers brace themselves against the seat in front
of them. Some ready barf bags.

Liv, sitting in the window seat, hyperventilates.

                              LIV
          This is it... I can see my whole life
          flashing before my eyes.

Victoria calmly braces herself against the seat in
front of her.

                              LIV
                    (shouting to passengers)
          Is there a priest on board? Anyone who
          knows how to give last rites?

                           VICTORIA
                  (off Liv)
          What are you doing? We're not even
          catholic.

                              LIV
          I want my rights!

Victoria mouths "SORRY" to a nearby passenger who
grew more anxious by Liv's question.

                              LIV
                  (off Victoria)
          It's all so clear now.

                           VICTORIA
          Liv –

                              LIV
          Mother... I need to die with a clear
          conscience.

                           VICTORIA
          Good grief.

                              LIV
          Last year, you gave me permission to
          sleep over at Carol's house for the
          weekend, but she told her parents she

                               80

was staying at our house... but really
we went to Vegas.

Victoria glares at Liv in shocking horror.

> LIV
> Mom, I'm so sorry. If I could go back
> and do it differently I potentially
> might.

> VICTORIA
> Who paid for - how did you -

> LIV
> Remember when your credit card got
> stolen?

Victoria glares wide-eyed at Liv.

Air masks fall from the ceiling. Liv SCREAMS.

> LIV
> I'm gonna die!

Victoria places a mask on her own face, then one onto
Liv's.

> LIV
> Mom... you've been the best mom in the
> world and I'm so thankful for you...
> even though it was totally unfair when
> you grounded me for a month in the
> tenth grade and I missed out on the
> ski-trip with -

Liv notices the air bag she's connected to has no
air.

> LIV
> I'm not getting any air! There's no
> air in my air thingy! Mom! I'm not
> getting any air!

                    VICTORIA
          In, two, three, out -

                      LIV
          There's nothing to breathe!

Liv appears to be suffocating.

                      LIV
          If you make it out of here, tell Dad
          and Tina I love them.

Liv GASPS for air.

                      LIV
               (her dying breath)
          My password is hashtag-yellow-forty-
          five.

Liv falls limp. Victoria breathes deeply, more
focused on coping with the stress of Liv, than by the
turbulence.

The plane settles to a calm. The FLIGHT ATTENDANTS
walk through the isles to check on the passengers.

                 FLIGHT ATTENDANT 1
               (off Victoria)
          You can take your mask off. It was
          just a precautionary measure. We
          didn't end up losing cabin pressure.

                    VICTORIA
          Thank you.

Victoria removes the mask. Liv opens one eye.

                    VICTORIA
          So... Vegas...

Liv sitting up, composed.

                    LIV
     It was a confession made under duress,
     Mom. You can't hold me to it.

Victoria narrows her eyes at Liv.

                    LIV
     It's literally illegal.

A passenger stumbles through the aisle and vomits on
Victoria. She freezes in shock.

                    LIV
     Gross.

Victoria looks up at a stewardess who offers a
sympathetic look.

My favorite part of writing is the characters. I love to come up with
what would be the most interesting personality to place in various
situations. I love to get to know them and then hear how they speak.
And I had an absolute blast writing the above scene.

Writers know what I mean by getting to know your characters, but if
you're not a writer, I'll do my best to explain. All of the various factors
of what makes each person unique influences how they interact with
the world around them. It dictates their decisions, speech patterns,
habits, and more. How a person thinks is who they really are. I don't
just decide that I want my character to say and do specific things. I
create a character and then get inside their head to understand how
they think. Once I know how they think, then they basically write
themselves.

For example, think about someone that you know really well and
consider how they would react in an emergency. Picture him/her at a

restaurant and an earthquake strikes. The ground shakes, the lights swing, suddenly everything is unstable and unpredictable. Can you see that scene play out clearly in your mind? Would your person freeze? Jump into action? Run away? Melt into a useless mess of tears?

There are a variety of ways that people respond in emergency situations. These responses are a reflection of their character. They don't have time to think and consider the best course of action, they have to respond immediately. They respond out of their already existing skills, history, belief system, etc. This is one of the exercises I use to get to know my characters.

I've learned that if I pay attention to people around me and truly listen to what they say, not just to hear the words, but to understand how they think, I can get a strong sense of their character and am able to predict their behavior with great accuracy.

One time, I was writing a radio commercial for a self-improvement seminar. I had already attended it myself and gotten to know the Director quite well. I figured since he was the one who led the majority of training sessions, I'd write the commercial for him to voice. When I sent him the script, he sent it to the founder of the company and her response was, "Well, you always had a way with words." When he told her he didn't write it, she was stunned. It sounded just like him. And when we recorded the commercial, it was as if his heart poured out through the mic. I had captured his unique voice because I understood his perspective and learned the nuance of his language.

One of the greatest life skills screenwriting has taught me is perspective-taking. As I mentioned, I create my characters and let them think for themselves, which means I have to allow myself to take-on their perspective. I must understand life through their lens in order to give them a voice. Now, transfer that skill to real live people. While I didn't create them, I am able to take in as many objective details as possible to develop a sense of their perspective. I listen to what they say to understand how they think. I watch their behavior and compare it with their words. I'm able to recognize, accept and adapt to the fact that people around me see the world differently than I do. There's not a single person in the world with a backstory identical to mine. No one has the same combination of attributes. I am unique... and so is everyone else in the world. And, therefore, so are each of our perspectives.

Because of this insight, I've learned how to listen to someone with an open mind and focus on understanding them regardless of whether I agree with or appreciate their point of view. I don't need to like a character (person) to understand their perspective. I don't need to agree with them to listen to the way they see things.

However, in this exercise of listening to learn, I'm also able to perceive subtext as I begin to understand how they think. Sometimes, a person can present one emotion, but actually be dealing with a different one. For example, a person who presents as angry or chaotic, may actually be anxious or afraid when you get to the heart of it. Of course, there are several other examples I could give you, but I've probably made my point; listening to learn, rather than listening to react, is an incredible life skill.

In order to change or mature my characters' perspectives, I send them on exactly the right journey and let them clash with other perspectives along the way. In the opening scene of *The Three Amigas*, we got to meet our characters in a high pressure situation.

We see Liv dealing with her intense anxiety and Victoria dealing with her intense daughter. Not only do we get to see that Liv has anxiety, but we also get to see that she lacks filters. She's willing to miss her sister's wedding, her emotions are all over the place, she admits to lying, and she's fairly self-centered. We can easily love her despite all of this, though. And clearly her mother loves her as well, despite the exhaustion of trying to navigate her daughter's needs and personality in a supportive and loving way. Liv is the perfect character to draw out Victoria's true character. In fact, Liv is going to play a big role in Victoria's character arc. And Victoria is the perfect character to draw out Liv's growth journey. But in order for that to happen, something needs to draw them out of their current dynamic. I need to throw a wrench into the mix. And I know the perfect character to challenge the status quo. (You'll get to meet Marly in the next chapter.)

Once I put these three characters in the same room, the sparks start to fly. But I don't stop there. I drop them into an undesirable situation with just the right amount of danger and tension so that what's in their hearts becomes exposed. With all their cards laid out on the table, they finally have what they need to each choose their character arc. Their perspective in the end will be different than at the start.

In elementary school, my son used to struggle with his emotions. He was impulsive when he was triggered. Once his patience was spent, whatever was within arms reach was thrown across the room. Sometimes, he'd lash out and hit someone if he felt they were picking on him.

I worked closely with the school to come up with a consistent approach to support him to overcome this character flaw; to pursue self-control. The school and I both saw the potential of who he could be if he was able to do so. We never pretended that his behavior wasn't a problem, but we very clearly spoke positive truth and expectation into his life. We gave him tools of how to manage himself in the situation and told him we believed he was capable of making good choices.

Then, one day, he was called to the office because he threatened to hit someone. When the principal asked for his version of the events, he said, "I wasn't going to hit him, I was just going to scare him. That's got to count for something!" I remember thinking that it was a small win on the way to a much bigger one, but we couldn't dismiss that he was starting to think differently. His perspective was changing. God was working on his character.

As God calls you into adventure and brings you from glory to glory, keep in mind that he's not trying to destroy your character, but rather to develop it deeper into who you were truly created to be. Sometimes, that means He needs to adjust your perspective. Don't be afraid to consider new ideas, or to take inventory of your lenses. God's not afraid of tough questions and in the end, if truth is what you seek, then the truth will stand firm.

Chapter 8
Goals and Crisis

Never let a good crisis go to waste. Winston Churchill

All stories revolve around a character having a goal. And all stories are driven by the writer having the goal to write about that character's journey. Goals are what keep us on track, allow us to measure our progress, and tell us when we've arrived. But something that often goes understated is how strongly goals motivate us.

This really hit home for me when I was helping families with special needs teens. I could see how motivated the family was to help their teen finish high school, but since I also had several years of experience working with adults with special needs, I also had the foresight to see that unless they created new goals for establishing adult life skills, they were going to achieve their goal of finishing school and then very quickly feel stuck and aimless.

This happens in marriages too. After the kids grow-up and move out, unless there's more to the relationship than achieving that specific goal, they begin to drift apart. Goals create a degree of resiliency in us to push through obstacles and difficulties. When we keep that goal in mind, we can make it through just about anything. That's amazing news and sobering news at the same time.

When you watch movies where people have to work together to achieve something, even though they don't like each other, you'll see that throughout the process, they end up gaining a respect, possibly even a desire, for one another.

This happens in life too. It's a great tool for fostering relationships and spending time and energy on someone. Think about when you're raising your kids. You can establish common goals with them to build the relationship and bond. As the parent, of course you want to use that opportunity to build beyond just the goal, but it's one of the best bonding tools you have available to you. You don't even need to be an expert.

When one of my sons was 14 years old, he told me he wanted to be a Youtuber. My instant inside reaction was to roll my eyes. He'd been begging for more and more computer time and I was telling him that he needed to work toward something creative. But I stopped myself from responding and heard him out. He wanted to play video games and make money on YouTube. Right. Okay.

So, I decided to support that decision. He wanted to build his own computer and I figured it'd be a good experience for him anyway. Instead of butting heads over this computer and his idea, we started enjoying the pursuit of the goal.

Of course, after a few months, he realized how much work it was and understood how challenging it'd be to achieve enough of an audience to make money at it and changed his mind, but the point is that sharing the goal allowed us to bond. And in the end, he chose for himself to set that aside, instead of me deciding for him.

However, had he continued with it, he would've learned a lot of other valuable skills and I would've been able to influence him in his choices because we shared the common goal. Had I dismissed his goal, he would've pursued it without me and I would've missed my opportunity. I'm not suggesting that every teen has goals worth pursuing, but sometimes it's best to let them have a go at it and see for themselves. That's when they learn. And if it happens that they fail, we're right there to bond with them during the crisis as well.

Crisis is another strong bonding opportunity. It's obvious that when we go through times of loss, defeat, intense struggle, or any other kind of crisis, we appreciate supportive social interaction more than usual. And when the connection comes from someone experiencing the same ordeal, it's even more meaningful and bonding.

Think about how communities rally together when there's been a natural disaster. There are a lot of natural disaster type movies where you can see this play out. People that either didn't know each other or didn't like each other, bond as they work together to survive. They grieve with one another and encourage each other. Crisis will reveal character more than build it, because we'll see people without their filters a lot of the time.

Remember *The Three Amigas*? Let's catch up with Liv and Victoria toward the end of Act 1. Since the airplane fiasco, they've arrived at the cruise for the wedding vacation, then disembarked for the day. We've also been introduced to Marley, the beautiful fiance of Victoria's ex-husband. Victoria has no desire to speak with Marly, let alone befriend her.

Scene from The Three Amiga's written by Jaclyn Whitt:

EXT. STREET MARKET - DAY

Victoria browses through the market and tries on a hat.

                    MARLY (O.C.)
              (pleasantly)
          It suits you.

Victoria turns to thank the person. It's Marly. Ugh.

Victoria replaces the hat and walks off.

Marly, offended and fed up, follows after her.

                    MARLY
          What's your problem? What did I ever
          do to you?

Liv, at a nearby vendor, notices them arguing.
Victoria walks faster, ignoring Marly. Marly keeps
pace.

                    MARLY
          Our daughters need us to get along!

Victoria, shocked, turns and glares at Marly.

                    VICTORIA
          OUR daughters? MY. Daughters.

                    MARLY
          Michael and I are getting married next
          month, so...

Victoria hesitates, stunned at the news, but refuses
to show vulnerability.

                    VICTORIA
          Show me your stretch marks. Tell me
          how Tina got the scar on her knee. How
          many school lunches did you pack?

Marly, humbled, glances away.

CARLOS, 40, a thief, eyes their purses and cautiously
moves closer to them.

                    VICTORIA (O.C.)
                (feigning sympathy)
        What? Did I say something to hurt your
        feelings?
                (vengeful)
        You're nothing but a cute little whim
        for Michael. It's embarrassing!

Liv, fed-up, storms over to the women, in Marly's
defense.

                    LIV
        What's your problem, Mom? Marly's
        totally extra.

Victoria glares at Marly and the two of them burst
into arguing over each other.

                    MARLY
        If I were a whim, he wouldn't have
        asked me to marry him!

                    VICTORIA
        You could never fill my shoes!

                    MARLY
        Really? What's Liv's boyfriend's name?

Liv glares at Marly.

                    VICTORIA
        Liv doesn't have a boy --

Marly smiles smugly.

Liv glances around looking guilty.

Victoria's eyes narrow on Liv, then back at Marly.

Carlos moves closer.

                    VICTORIA
          How old was she when she cut her first
          tooth? Who taught her to swim?

                    MARLY
          How did Tina and Ricky meet? I bet you
          don't know the real story!

                    LIV
               (off Victoria)
          You don't.

Carlos grabs their purses and runs off. The three
women shift gears and run after the thief.

                    VICTORIA
          Hey! Thief!

                    MARLY
          Stop him!

Carlos hops over a table and down an alley.

                    VICTORIA
               (off Marly while running)
          This is all your fault!

                    MARLY
          Seriously?

Victoria and Marly climb over the table and keep
running.

                    MARLY
          If you weren't so determined to hate
          me for no reason, it never would've --

                    VICTORIA
          I have plenty reason!

Carlos crosses a busy street, narrowly avoiding a
car.

The women follow, running through traffic, SQUEALING in fear.

                    MARLY
        What could you possibly have against
        me?

                    VICTORIA
        You're not good enough for my husband
        or daughters!

Marly stops just in time to avoid running into a bicycle.

                    MARLY
        Ex-husband!

Victoria and Liv close in on the thief.

Marly re-joins the pursuit.

Carlos turns a corner.

Victoria and Liv follow.

Marly catches up and turns the corner only to stop dead in her tracks, wide-eyed.

Victoria and Liv stand defensively in the middle of a group of THUGS in a back alley. They all turn to Marly.

Marly glances between the group and the empty road she just came from.

ALVARO, 35, leader of the thugs, steps toward Marly.

                    ALVARO
                (Speaking Spanish)
        Give it up, girl. Game over.

Marly, not understanding, glances around, panicked.

                    ALVARO
          (Amused, Speaking Spanish)
     You don't speak Spanish? Huh? Pretty
     thing?

He struts over to Marly.

                    MARLY
     I don't - I don't understand.
     Please... please, just let us go.

Victoria listens intently.

Carlos steps forward.

                    CARLOS
          (Speaking Spanish)
     Let 'em go, man. We got what we need.

                    ALVARO
          (Speaking Spanish)
     This one's cute, though, eh? Look at
     those curves.

He winks at Marly and checks her out. Marly tries to
cover her cleavage.

                    ALVARO
          (Regarding Liv)
     We could make good money with the
     young one.

Victoria's eyes widen.

                    CARLOS
          (Speaking Spanish)
     That's too far, man... I don't want
     any real trouble here. Just let them
     go.

                    ALVARO
              (reluctantly giving in)
          Tch.

He turns to one of the guys and motions toward some
rope.

                    ALVARO
              (Speaking Spanish)
          Tie them up.

Marly roundhouse kicks Alvaro in the head and knocks
him out. Marly, surprised at herself and high on
adrenaline, stares at him a moment.

Victoria, Liv and the thugs stare at Marly, jaw-
dropped.

                    LIV
          That was totally bad-ass.

Marly takes a fighting stance.

Liv grabs her phone from her back pocket and records
it on video.

Marly does a knee, kick, jab, punch combo.

                    MARLY
          Who's next!?

The men stare at one another, confused and amused.

                    MARLY
          C'mon! ... I'ma kick all your gluteus
          maximuses! Who's next, huh? Who wants
          a piece of me!?

She slightly advances, doing a jab, jab, cross-body
punch.

The men take a step back, stifling laughter.

Victoria shoots Marly a "What are you doing?" look.

                         MARLY
                    (off the thugs)
              What are ya, chicken? Huh? Pollo!

Marly walks around, CLUCKING like a chicken.

The men look at each other and burst out laughing.

Liv, recording video, laughs with the guys as if
they're all in on the same joke.

                          LIV
                   Right? So extra.

Victoria sees an opportunity, grabs Liv's arm and
runs off.

The thugs attempt to follow but Marly steps in front
of them.

Screaming, Marly does a few uppercuts and a
roundhouse, then follows after Victoria and Liv,
running like a crazy woman.

Victoria, Liv and Marly high tail it down the road,
back to the market area.

They enter the market, still screaming and slow to a
stop, once in a populated area, heaving to catch
their breath.

Liv bursts out laughing.

                          LIV
              That was the best thing I've ever seen
              in my life! This is gonna go viral.

Liv works on her phone.

                    VICTORIA
            (off Marly)
        What was that?

                    MARLY
            (bragging)
        Part of my fitness repertoire... I
        teach kickboxing on Thursdays.

Marly curtsies.

                    VICTORIA
        Oh no! What time is it?

                    LIV
        Who cares? We're on vacation.

Marly clues in.

                    MARLY
        The ship!

And they're off! They all run through the town in a
panic.

This is what starts their journey together. These three ladies will very soon realize that they've missed getting back on board the cruise ship and will have to travel together to meet up with the boat at the next port. They'll have a common goal in the midst of a crisis situation which will cause them to continuously learn about each other and eventually be able to make appropriate judgments of one another, not just ones based on emotional triggers and assumptions.

Ready for the big question? Is it possible that God is allowing a crisis in your life to cause you and the people in your life to have to work together? Even if you don't like each other, or want to like each other, your Author may have other plans. And if you're going through a crisis with people you already love, how will you get through it? No one is ever the same on the other side of a crisis. Will you grow together or apart?

Crisis is never something to be hoped for, but when it strikes, we can have confidence in our Author that he's able to get us through it. Most likely, you're not alone in the situation. Others are suffering, too. Lean on each other instead of blaming each other.

If ever there was a time to love others as you would want to be loved, a crisis would be the time to do it. Be quick to forgive and quick to ask for forgiveness. Extending grace to one another, especially during a crisis, allows for trust to build. It's a situation that can make or break relationships.

Sometimes, it may seem like a risky move for God to allow such a difficult situation. It doesn't just test relationships with people in our lives, but it can test our relationship with our own Author. Some people get angry at God or walk away from their faith because of a crisis. I admit there were times where I felt like my pain was unfair. That's when the Holy Spirit would remind me of the conversation between Jesus and his disciples in John 6:67-68.

After Jesus' teachings were too difficult, many people who were following him walked away. Jesus turned to his disciples and asked if they wanted to leave him, too. Simon Peter responded, "Lord, where else would we go? You're the one with the answers."

The Holy Spirit would ask me, "Do you want out of this relationship?"

And I would always respond the same way Simon Peter did.

If your crisis is testing your faith, I invite you to remember this. It's not just a statement of resolve, but of hope. Jesus is the one with the answers.

Chapter 9
Does Life Have a Genre?

I have a theory.

Every life has drama. But do you actually live in a drama? How would you even know? It may surprise you to discover that it's not so simple to feel the genre of your life while you're living it.

As mentioned previously, in order to achieve your character arc, you'll have to go through a learning process that comes with a lot of failure and frustration. This is across the board, no matter the genre. Don't believe me? Watch a comedy and see how the hero feels at around 30 minutes into the film. No doubt you're laughing your head off while he's completely freaking out. He's not laughing. He doesn't feel like he's in a comedy. And neither will you at the time.

So, why bring this up? What does it even matter? Well, I have a theory. I think that if we look back and assess the patterns of our lives, and how we feel about them, we can gain some valuable insights.

COMEDY

How many times have you told a crazy story about your past that you were laughing while telling, but at the time it was happening, you were definitely not laughing? Like, at the time, you were legit freaking out, scared, stressed, or frustrated. If your life is a series of these kinds of stories, it's likely your life is a comedy. It's full of crazy ups and downs that you can look back and laugh at. If you don't have many or any of these stories, then maybe your life isn't a comedy. But I'm sure you know of someone who is like this.

Oftentimes, people in this genre are adventurous. This doesn't necessarily mean they go on wild, extreme vacations or missions, although they might. But it means they're willing to step outside their comfort zone. Wait, let me rephrase that. They're not always willing in the sense of seeking out opportunities to live outside their comfort zone, but rather, when the situation presents itself, they're in before they realize what they've gotten themselves into. Not only do they regularly find themselves in over their heads, but they've got a lot of thoughts and emotions.

While this genre may reveal some impulsivity and naivety, the person's ability to look back and laugh at the craziness that regularly consumes their life is what sets them apart from other genres. Stand-up comedians are great at sharing stories from their lives in a way that only a comedian could do. They're able to take all kinds of undesirable situations and frame it in a way that makes it enjoyable to look back on. We all face humiliation, danger, awkwardness, etc. in life. But not all of us are able to look back and find the funny.

It's fun to find comedy in the Bible. 1 Kings chapter 18 is one of my favorite stories.

EXT. FIELD - DAY

Obadiah walks along, minding his own business.

> ELIJAH (O.S.)
> Hey, man.

Obadiah looks over to see Elijah walking toward him.

                    OBADIAH
          Elijah? Is it really you?

Obadiah glances around, nervously.

                    ELIJAH
          Yeah, I got back this morning. Go tell
          the king.

                    OBADIAH
          Are you kidding me? You think I got a
          death wish or something?

                    ELIJAH
          What are you talking about?

                    OBADIAH
          As soon as I report to the king, God's
          going to send you somewhere else and
          I'm gonna be left to answer for your
          disappearance. No way. You go tell him
          yourself.

Elijah CHUCKLES and gestures for Obadiah to go.

                    OBADIAH
          Haven't I been good to you? To God?
          I've been hiding you guys and feeding
          you… I'm doing all I can, but if I say
          you're back and then you're not here…

                    ELIJAH
          No worries, man. It's time for me and
          Ahab to have a little chat. I'm not
          going anywhere.

Obadiah stares Elijah down, searching his eyes while
he works to process a decision.

Elijah shoots him a mischievous smile.

Obadiah EXHALES heavily.

LATER

King Ahab descends from his chariot, barely able to
keep himself from tripping over his over-extravagant
robes.

He approaches Elijah, nose in the air… because
otherwise his crown would fall off his head.

> KING AHAB
> Well, well, well… if it isn't…
>> (searches for a word)
> …the trouble-maker. Yes, you trouble-
> maker of Israel.

> ELIJAH
> I'm the trouble-maker? You're the one
> leading God's people astray. He's not
> happy about that, by the way.

> KING AHAB
> Why are you here this time? Are you
> going to turn off…
>> (searches for the words)
> …the-the-the sun? Mmm?

> ELIJAH
> The Almighty One of Israel wants a
> showdown with your false god, Baal.

> KING AHAB
> False god!?

> ELIJAH
> Oh, and the prophets of your crazy
> wife's god are also invited.

Incredulity floods Ahab's face and he starts
STAMMERING.

                    ELIJAH
     Cheer-up, it'll be good times. See-you
     tomorrow.

Elijah pats King Ahab's shoulder and walks off
without looking back.

King Ahab STAMMERS, searching for a come-back.

                    KING AHAB
     Not if I see you first.

Obadiah hides his amusement and King Ahab awkwardly
climbs back onto his chariot.

Okay, so clearly that was my version of the events. But what's crazy is that after Elijah confronts the prophets of Baal on Mount Carmel, taunting them to call out louder to their god and then calling fire down from heaven, Elijah has an emotional meltdown the next day. Like it finally hit him what just happened. Highs and lows! In it before he knows what's good for him. My guess is that when we meet Elijah in heaven, he'll be doing stand-up as he recounts his life.

It's not all fun and games, though. Depending on the temperament of the people around the person whose life is a comedy, they can be perceived in a number of ways.

Some people will enjoy them and know there will never be a dull moment. But not everyone is able to manage the rollercoaster. Some won't understand them and will only see their impulsivity and naivety. They'll look down on them and wonder if they'll ever grow-up, hence the constant question that comedians face, "When are you going to get a real job?" Others will enjoy them in small amounts. These people love to hear the stories after everything's been resolved, but they're not up for watching the craziness play out in real time.

People in this genre can feel on top of the world one moment and completely misunderstood and misjudged the next. If all this resonates with you and you think you're living in a comedy genre, then be patient with the variety of ways that people perceive you. It's not easy to live in a comedy. Things go wrong regularly, pretty much one thing after another. Your life may exhaust some people, but your ability to look back and laugh is a blessing to you and everyone around you.

DRAMA

While even a comedy has serious, dramatic moments, it's nothing compared to the weightier feeling of a drama. Yes, there will be comedic moments during a drama as well, but the approach to telling the story is more on the serious side. Some subject matter and situations demand it to be so. Sobering issues like addiction, trauma, abuse, and so on, are told in dramas, not comedies. If your life revolves around more serious issues, then you're likely living in a drama.

There will be seasons in life where we find ourselves caught up in a dramatic story. For some it may only be for a few months or years, and then they settle back into their typical genre. But for some, this seems to be the running theme of their life.

The most important thing to understand is that the hero of a drama often feels alone in their struggle. They might even create that situation by pushing people away. If you watch dramatic movies, watch what the heroes do to make their life harder than necessary and then check yourself to see if you do the same. Assess the lies that the hero is believing, then ask yourself what lies you're believing. You can learn a lot about yourself by assessing characters, especially the ones that irritate you. If you're like me, it'll irritate you to see negative traits in others because they're the exact same traits you have but are doing your best to ignore.

How you deal with your life situations and what you do on the other side of the journey will point to whether you fall into the inspirational genre or not.

People who get through a disaster by the skin of their teeth and just keep moving forward without sharing their story don't fit into this category. But if they're compelled by their gratitude and healing to share their journey, despite having to point out their own failures, in order to encourage others in the same situation, then they're living an inspirational life. Some people just can't help but tell the world what they've been through. Despite it being embarrassing, shameful, or horrific, the healing on the other side is too incredible to keep quiet about. They may express this on a grand scale by writing a book, speaking publicly about it, or they might just be always ready to share their story with a friend of a friend who needs to hear it.

These people have been through a lot. They healed enough to find purpose and meaning in their past. They've accepted that it is what it is and that they couldn't be who they are today without having gone through it. In this situation, you'll see that attitude makes all the difference. They could easily fall into the drama genre, but they've taken it further and pressed on into inspiration.

ROMANCE

Some people just love "love". Who wouldn't want to have that ongoing thrill and excitement of falling in love? Unfortunately, the sad part about the romance genre is that it's always about the pursuit of love. Once the hero finds love, the journey is over. As much as we imagine that the person living in a romance genre has a satisfying and exciting life, what they really have is a constant pursuit of what they believe will complete them. Now, I love a good romcom, I even write romcoms, but I don't want to live in one. It's fine for a season, but if you find your life seems to be a constant pursuit of romance and intimacy, you may have swallowed the lie of, "...and they lived happily ever after."

It doesn't matter how amazing of a partner you find, if you expect him/her to complete you, you'll find yourself dissatisfied. We all have something inside us that longs for connection. We search for people that can draw out certain parts of ourselves regarding intellect, humor, spirituality. We foster relationships that provide comfort, grace, and love. But there are two specific relationship dynamics that are different from all else; a relationship with a spouse and a relationship with our Creator.

One of the things that makes God amazing is that he placed both of these longings within each one of us. Each relationship has its place and we need to be careful that we don't try to fit our spouse into the role that only our Creator was designed to fulfill. God placed it in our DNA to need him in a way that can't be satisfied by anything earthly. It's the part of us that we don't fully understand, yet remains a strong motivating force in our lives. Some people try to fill it with drugs, career, art, family... and romance. Whatever we're trying to fill that God-sized hole with can give us some sense of purpose and identity for a time, but they can't actually fulfill either one.

Only God can give us our true purpose and identity. It was a harsh reality check when I discovered that although the romantic genre was alluring, it was empty in the end.

If you want to break out of the cycle of constantly pursuing romance, it starts with recognizing what you're truly searching for so you can fill it with the only thing that can truly satisfy you.

The woman at the well in John 4:5-30, is a perfect example. She was living in the romance genre. She'd had several partners, some of whom were apparently affairs with men she wasn't married to. Jesus pointed out to her that the water she was drinking would always leave her thirsty again, but that the water he was offering her would finally satisfy her so that she would never thirst again. The answer to finding a fulfilling long term relationship is in proper compartmentalization. God is God. A partner is a partner. Don't get them confused.

DRAMEDY

What about people who seem to have a strong combination of both comedy and drama? We call this "dramedy". It's exactly what it sounds like; a good balance of drama and comedy. I feel like a lot of people fall into this category.

This is my favorite genre to write because it seems to reflect life really well. Plus, as a writer, I like to have the freedom to bounce between a variety of emotions over and over again.

If you feel like you have a strong balance of both genres, then my only advice for you is to enjoy and endure. You have an opportunity to have some amazingly beautiful moments, but they'll sometimes come at a cost. Be careful not to miss out on fully cherishing those joys just because you know that struggle is around the corner. Don't let the drama steal your laughter. Do the reverse. When you're in those tough times, remember to laugh in the midst of it.

A person who lives in the genre of dramedy is able to find a reason to laugh, or at least chuckle, even in the midst of struggle and sorrow. They won't bring levity to avoid dealing with the situation, but rather because they know the facts of life - they take the good, they take the bad. (If you didn't catch that joke, ask a Gen-X'er.)

HORROR

Horror sucks and I hope this isn't you. It means exactly what it says. Some people are in a situation where they are literally running for their life for pretty much their whole life. They have no idea what's around the next turn. They have no idea if and when help will arrive. All they can do is pay attention to everything and see if they can find patterns and vulnerabilities in their oppressor.

This genre causes people to become hyper vigilant and discerning. That's what they need if they're going to make it out alive. There may have been a season in your life when you lived through a horror story. First, I want to say that I'm sorry you went through that. If you're still dealing with the trauma of that situation, all I can suggest is to assess your life as a whole, recognize that episode for what it was and how it affected you, and trust your Author to lead you toward healing and wholeness.

Hopefully, you won't have to sit with your back against the far wall at every restaurant your whole life. I pray that you can once again do the things you used to do, that your tongue would not stutter and your heart not race. May you have victory over the nightmares.

TRAGEDY

Tragedy is a mixed bag. Before tragedy can strike, beauty must first be present. If your life is a cycle of loss of loved ones, stolen opportunities, and unfair rejection, then you understand suffering, and I'm sorry for your loss. But what you also uniquely understand is the value of value itself. You can only experience loss by first having.

To miss a person so deeply you can't breathe, or to feel like the weight of your heart is beyond what you can bear, is to understand how to place deep value on a person. If you're in the midst of it right now, it might be too soon to grasp this, but if you can look back and see how beautiful your heart is to value so deeply, you can turn your grief into gratitude. The grief will always be there and sometimes you'll need to sit with it. That's true. But if you can see the gift of having what you had, realizing that some never even have that depth of connection, desire, or passion.

A story is only tragic because we understand what could've been and because the emotions are deep. Many artists who have lived a tragic life created incredible songs, paintings, and stories. Not everyone in the world knows how to experience that level of emotions. Some run from them or deny them. But art has a way of calling emotions forth and leading an emotionally reluctant person into feeling. If and when you're ready to share your story, there are people who long to hear the depths of your journey. The tragedy genre is often combined with either drama or inspiration. Attitude is the determining factor for this combination.

There are several other genres, like action, thriller, sci-fi, adventure, etc. But all of those genres and others will be in combination with the above genres. If you're in law enforcement, you might consider that your life is an action genre. But then, I'd challenge you by asking, "Action what?" Comedy, drama, dramedy, romance...?

"What if I don't like my genre? Can I change it?" Well, I have a theory. I strongly believe that because we have free will, and because the genre is often determined by perspective and attitude, then I believe we have the ability to change our genre. I've done my best to offer insights into the various perspectives. If you feel like you fall into one category, but want to shift to another, then see what the life and attitude of the desired genre is. If you can adopt this new perspective and attitude, then you can begin to shift the course/genre of your life.

You'll also need to embrace the realities of that genre. For example, comedy journeys are funny when we look back, but typically not while we're going through them. So, in order for you to look back and laugh, you have to learn to not take yourself too seriously. You'll need to accept that you won't always be laughing. You'll probably end up in embarrassing, dangerous, or awkward situations.

These are fantastic stories to tell AFTER enough time has gone by. But you will have to first go through them, then heal and learn to laugh, then be ready to tell people so you can enjoy the comedic journey of life. There are stories I've heard from such people where they both laugh and shudder at their past. They would never choose to go through that again. But they're able to laugh at it and invite others to laugh with them. So, choose wisely.

Sometimes, life just happens and you have no choice but to deal with it. A horror isn't going to change into a comedy overnight. But just because you're in one genre at the moment, it doesn't mean you're designated to be that way for your entire life. You may even be able to look back at seasons of your life and easily label them, even if your life is nothing like that now.

My goal with this chapter is to invite you to think deeply about patterns and perspective, and to raise your awareness. How your story plays out, how you process your emotions, is between you and your Author. If you're in the middle of a storm right now, I encourage you to prayerfully ask God what kind of story he wants to tell through you in this situation. When you ask in humility and surrender, and listen for that still, small voice, you might be amazed at what you hear.

Chapter 10
The Depths of Music

What's the soundtrack to your life?

Music is part of the human experience. All cultures throughout history have created music. While some animals seem to also appreciate music, humans seem to enjoy it to a greater degree. We craft a variety of musical instruments and proceed to compose musical phrases, movements and songs, combining music, story and emotion together. Different rhythms, melodies, harmonies, and even dissonant notes can grip our emotions and hold them at will.

I've always been a huge fan of music. I can't help but move when I hear a good beat. Did you know that studies show that music connects with the part of our brain that facilitates coordination and movement? While I didn't take dance lessons until my young adult years, music always inspired me to move. It's part of why I became a group fitness instructor and why I taught a praise dance class for kids.

Not only does music make me want to move, but it does it in such a way that my emotions match the intent of the emotions within the song. Praise music touches my heart so deeply that I've been told by people that they love to watch me dance because it's not just my body that's moving, but my spirit rejoicing. I'm not the most versatile or incredible dancer by any stretch of the imagination, but I am authentic and free. Music removes my defenses. It's not uncommon for me to be the first person on the dance floor.

Not only can stories be told through music, but music can drum up emotions while hearing or watching a scenario play out. One of the beautiful things about movies is the capacity to incorporate a multitude of artistic mediums all at the same time.

Great dialogue and acting can be moving in and of itself, but throw in a talented cinematographer and film scorer and I'm easily turned into a mess of snot tears. Even just one note on a piano (the right note) can help the audience connect with the internal struggle of the character without the actor saying a word or shifting in the slightest. It's as if music is an invisible character, like a spirit, that connects one dimension to another.

Imagine your favorite movie with a completely different soundtrack. Would it be the same? Just for fun, someone made a trailer for the movie Elf. They changed up the soundtrack and presented it as a horror/thriller movie instead of a family comedy. You can find it on Youtube by searching for "Elf recut as a Thriller." It's hilarious. Music is one of the most important pieces in fulfilling the film genre. The wrong music can push it into another genre entirely.

What about you? What songs are in the soundtrack of your life? If you struggled to figure out your genre in the last chapter, maybe this chapter can help you determine it. What kind of music do you listen to? What are the messages contained within them? Do you listen to songs of hope, praise, beauty, partying, depression, sensuality, disrespect? If you read the lyrics to your favorite songs, can you respect them? Can the lyrics represent you and your beliefs? Or do they contradict who you believe yourself to be, or who you are working to become? What invisible character do you give permission to, to connect you to another dimension? I know that might sound like a crazy question, and perhaps even a total nutter of an idea, but follow me...

There's something called "music memory"; the part of our brain that stores music. I know I'm not the only one who can hear three notes of a song I haven't heard in 30+ years only to realize I still recall the entire song by heart. (Of course, then it's stuck in my head for a week.) Even Alzheimer's and head injury patients who've lost a vast amount of their memory can still remember music. In the documentary Alive Inside, which I encourage you to watch, filmmaker Michael Rossato-Bennett follows social worker Dan Cohen for three years in Dan's mission to deliver ipods to patients with dementia.

When we first meet these patients, most of them are completely disengaged with the world around them. But when Dan plays a song from their younger years, the patient becomes alive. Henry, a man who couldn't carry on much of a conversation, could sing every word of "I'll be Home for Christmas."

Another patient, John, couldn't recognize his younger self in a photo, but he was able to sing along with old songs. And, not only did it trigger his memory to recall lyrics, but suddenly he was telling stories of his life from those years. The music literally unlocked long lost memories.

Music activates more parts of our brain than anything else, recording itself into our memories, emotions, and coordination. But these patients didn't have the same response to every type of music, just the music they had enjoyed in their younger years. They connected with the soundtrack of their own lives.

Below is a scene from the documentary, Alive Inside. I've given the husband and wife fictitious names for the sake of making it simpler and more engaging to read.

115

INT. NURSING HOME - DAY

MARTY, (70'S) lost in his own world of dementia, sits across from his wife, DONNA (70's) who waits with bated breath for a moment with the man who once knew her.

He listens to MUSIC through his headphones.

                    MARTY
          Good song.

Donna smiles, cautiously optimistic, and stretches her hand towards him.

                    DONNA
          Can we hold hands a little bit?

Marty reaches out and takes her hand.

                    DONNA
          Aww, that's better. We're too far from
          each other.

While he's still in his own world, the music's got his attention. The song "CAN'T TAKE MY EYES OFF OF YOU" plays in his headphones.

                    MARTY
               (singing along)
          Can't take my eyes off of you...

INT. INTERVIEW ROOM - DAY

DR. OLIVER SACKS, MD, neurologist, author, shares his heartfelt expertise.

                    DR. SACKS
     For the patients with Alzheimers, it
     has to be music which has meaning for
     them and is correlated with memory and
     feeling.

INT. NURSING HOME - DAY

Marty sways to the music, which Donna can hear
faintly from her side of the table, but he's still
not making a connection with her.

                    DONNA
              (singing along)
     I want to hold you so much.

Longing fills her eyes.

INT. INTERVIEW ROOM - DAY

DR. CONNIE TOMAINO, Executive Director for the
Institute for Music and Neurologic Function, shares
her expertise.

                    DR. CONNIE
     And by exciting or awakening those
     pathways, we have a gateway to
     stimulate and reach somebody who is
     otherwise unreachable.

INT. NURSING HOME - DAY

Marty looks at his wife, as if waking up.

                    MARTY
     Yeah, it's not an easy life for you.

Acknowledgement flashes in his eyes.

                    MARTY
     I love you.

Now, with her husband fully cognizant and present,
Donna's tears flow freely.

                    DONNA
          I love you, too.

A husband and wife are reunited and enjoy their
moment together.

Music psychology reveals that music is able to connect with the limbic system which is deep in the human brain. Music also connects with the brain's pleasure and reward center. Have you ever listened to a song that gripped your emotions?

(Confession: I can't listen to the Christmas Shoes song. "I want her to look beautiful if Mama meets Jesus tonight..." Not gonna cry! Not gonna cry!) That's because music connects with the highly emotional and primitive parts of the brain. Just like storytelling, music is able to create and resolve tension. It does this in patterns that walk the fine line between the unexpected and predictable. Too unexpected and it'll turn most people off. Too predictable and it'll sound immature, hokey, or boring.

Does music reflect our mood? Or does our mood respond to the music? Yes and yes. We can choose music based on the mood we're in; when our hearts are breaking, we tend to choose music that helps us to feel like we're not alone in that emotion. But it's also true that we can use music to shift our mood.

In my mid-20's I suffered from pretty severe depression. I tried medication. I put a lot of effort into choosing the right diet. I intentionally dressed nicely and put make-up on. I exercised, forced myself to get out of bed, and spent time outside in the fresh air. I did as many things as I could think of to feel better and pull myself out of the depression.

But the thing that made the absolute biggest difference for my sense of well-being was choosing to listen to upbeat music. I chose songs that I was familiar with that had brought me joy in the past, that caused me to sing along with them, and inspired me to move. I could go from barely being able to force a smile to smiling inside and out by the time the chorus hit. It was fleeting, but it proved to me that I was still capable of joy; it wasn't lost forever.

At that time, I used to hear demonic voices that would tell me to pursue destructive behaviors. These voices would try to convince me they were my own thoughts. They'd tell me to take up drinking, start smoking, start a drug habit, try cutting, etc., as if it would offer relief in some way. (Yeah, we just got deep.) Anytime I had these "thoughts", I would consider them and end with the conclusion that it would just complicate my life further. (Had my parents not raised me to think through decisions logically, I might've followed through on the ideas.)

But just because I chose to make a logical choice, didn't mean those voices let up. In my case, I had to realize some difficult truths and find deliverance through Christ to finally resolve my depression. But during that oppression, music could stop the voices. Music did what medicine and will-power could not. It connected with me on a deeper level because that's what music does in the brain and in the spirit.

In my younger years, I would move to music without a single thought as to whether I agreed with the message or not. I started to realize that certain rhythms called for certain physical movements. Certain instruments would inspire specific parts of my body. Some songs would have me moving my feet while others my hips or shoulders. Some I would feel led to bounce to while others, I'd prefer to glide across the floor. A polka, for example, brings out very different movements than a waltz. Latin rhythms versus grunge. Take your pick, each one seems to draw on specific emotions and movements. In my late 20's, as part of walking out my salvation, I came to realize that I had a responsibility to discern music and how I interacted with it.

Music is more powerful than we're able to understand. Throughout history, cultures have used music as part of spiritual rituals. The Bible even speaks of music affecting the spiritual realm. In 1 Samuel chapter 16, Saul finds himself being tormented by an evil spirit and sends his attendants to find a musician who can play the harp and, therefore, relieve his burden. David, son of Jesse, was brought in to play for Saul. The end of chapter 16 states that whenever the evil spirit would come upon Saul, David would play his harp and it would relieve Saul. But more importantly, it also states that the evil spirit would leave him. How could playing the harp cause a spirit to respond in any way?

In Ephesians 5:15-20, the writer gives cautionary advice to the congregation. He states what to stay away from (drunkenness, which leads to debauchery) and what to embrace (singing hymns to one another and in your heart) in order to give thanks to the Lord and guard yourself from sin.

You can read about the fall of Jericho in Joshua 6 and Gideon's army of trumpeters in Judges 7. Whenever the Israelites went out into battle, who led the troops? The musicians. The praise and worship leaders led the charge. They worshiped their God, connecting to the spiritual realm in His holy name, while they encouraged each other in the Lord. There's something spiritual about music that we can't fully comprehend. We can, however, discern it.

Throughout my childhood, I was in several bands and choirs and I always loved feeling the vibrations from all directions, as I was in the middle of the music. I also loved the fact that several people were playing together, each with their own distinct part, to create a cohesive experience for the audience. The bonding sense of coordinated unity is hard to explain or replicate.

One of the things I'm most looking forward to when I enter eternity is corporate worship. We will finally have a genre that resonates with everyone. Can you imagine how amazing it's going to be when there are millions of believers from across space and time singing together in one accord? I can't even imagine the joy and awe it'll inspire when we're all together, with our King at the center, singing with complete freedom and shalom. The beauty of the thought alone is enough to draw a tear.

Chapter 11
Bad Guys

Villains, Anti-heroes, and Gatekeepers

We all have those characters we love to hate. The adversary, villain, bad guy, opponent, opposition, enemy, antagonist, etc... These are all words to describe one of the most important characters in a story. But are all adversaries evil? How do I know who the adversary is? Can an adversary become a good guy in the end? The answers are: No. Let's talk. That's up for debate.

One of the things that can make a story complex is the fact that not all adversaries are evil. It's easy to know who the bad guy is when he really is a rotten apple. But an adversary could be just a worthy opponent. In competition-themed movies, the adversary could be an intimidating rival. The sports team, cheerleaders, or musicians, from the other school aren't necessarily evil students. But if the hero's goal is to win, then his opponent is the one who wants the hero to lose.

That's how you know who the adversary is. When you boil it down, the adversary is the one who is the most invested in preventing the hero from achieving his goal. The adversary's behavior itself will depend on how the writer decides to write him. Sometimes, the adversary can actually gain the audience's sympathy, which creates wonderful complexity because it's not so cut and dry. In the end, the hero who achieves his character arc will have the ability to face his adversary unintimidated.

But what if the adversary isn't obvious? It's true that an adversary may not be obvious in the first half of the movie. You may only be able to clearly identify who he is as we progress toward the crisis moment.

Many times, this is when the adversary is actually invested in preventing the hero from achieving their character arc. They may fully support the hero's original goal, which, in time, the audience discovers would be the hero's demise. In this situation, it's more like the adversary in the story is actually an adversary of the author.

A hero could, in the beginning, have a goal that opposes the author's goal. The author has to actually grab his attention enough to get the hero to change his pursuit.

In this case, the adversary might be a friend who supported the hero's original goal. As the hero changes, the adversary doesn't, which is how he becomes the adversary, and his true colors are eventually revealed. This kind of bad guy would've been happy to have kept his friend on the path that leads to destruction, or to at least maintain the status quo. He's on the side of the hero as long as the hero is headed in the direction that is contrary to the author's plan. As the hero gains awareness of, and an inclination toward, the author's plan, he begins to pursue his character arc. This "friend" will turn on him, or encourage and support him back toward his original pursuit.

It's only after the midpoint, when the hero has a revelation that shifts his goal to be in line with the author's, that the "friend" becomes the one who is the most invested in preventing that goal from coming to fruition. The villain is actually the author's adversary and forces the hero to choose loyalties. In the end, the hero will have to break free of that relationship in order to pursue their own character arc.

Let's bring that into real life. The fact is that sometimes, there's a clear adversary in your life. There's someone who is preventing you from pursuing or achieving your goal. They create all kinds of obstacles and trouble. But also, sometimes there are people who appear to be on your side, but in reality, are keeping you from growing. This gets complicated because relationships, soul ties, and emotions are complex. It takes discernment for the hero to recognize the villain.

The Bible says that Satan masquerades as an angel of light. (2 Corinthians 11:14) It also gives a warning to watch out for wolves in sheep's clothing. (Matthew 7:15) But if you, as the hero of your story, truly believe that the Author loves you and knows you better than you know yourself, you can endure the pain and struggle of losing people and relationships.

The crisis moment is real. It's painful. It's never something I look forward to. But it's where growth happens. Like a bird who has to fight its way out of its shell and break free from the only world it's ever known, we must break through the walls (and people) that stifle our growth.

For people who want to change their lifestyle, it may mean they have to give up best friends. Those friends that don't have that same goal of change can be a stumbling block. At some point, the addict will have to break free of the relationship with his dealer or party friends because it's not conducive to him achieving his new goal.

Originally, his goal was to get high, have fun, escape responsibility, escape difficult emotions, be in a relationship, etc. But now, he wants a new life. Not only is he going to have to face all the things he was avoiding, but he's going to have to establish new routines. Part of the process will mean he must leave his old life and relationships behind him. This is never easy. There were legitimate good times and bonding experiences that happened. The connection and friendship is hard to walk away from. But in order to pursue a different life, it's what he must do.

A new Christian who has lived their life either in a different faith or in a lifestyle that is in opposition to Biblical values is faced with difficult decisions. He may need to separate himself from events or people for the same reason as the addict above. The reality is that we most often end up behaving like the people around us, so choose your friends wisely.

But what if the hero *is* the bad guy? According to the Oxford dictionary, an anti-hero is: A central character in a narrative or drama who lacks the admirable qualities of fortitude, courage, honesty, and decency that are usually possessed by traditional heroes.

Anti-heroes can be incredibly complex given that they're able to gain sympathy from an audience while doing things that the audience does not approve of. Complex or not, there are several ways to approach an anti-hero, and as always, there's a lot we can glean from understanding them.

One type of anti-hero is the character who wants so desperately to do the right thing, but keeps finding himself doing the wrong thing. An easy example of this type of situation is an addict whose addiction is in full swing. Even if he doesn't want to continue in his addiction, he keeps finding himself there. This leads to other destructive behaviors such as stealing from loved ones to support his habit. He knows it'll hurt them and break the trust in their relationship, but his need for the drugs is stronger.

In a movie, we can sympathize, knowing that it's not what the character really wants, because maybe the character also shared half of his sandwich, the only meal he got that day, with a homeless person. We can see his humanity, but he serves his flaw sacrificially.

He's listening to an inner voice that's telling him he has no choice. (Read those last two sentences again. Let it sink in.)

For the anti-hero, life can only end one of two ways: Either he changes which voice he listens to (thus no longer living as an anti-hero) or the flaw consumes him entirely (which is what happens in movies with anti-heroes).

Let me take a moment to clarify "destructive traits" because I'm not referring to character flaws. With destructive traits, the hero is fully aware of it and chooses to pursue it anyway because it serves him in some way, even at the expense of morality, legality, or how it affects his future and others around him. There can be some gray areas between the two, but as we continue, I hope you'll understand how to identify the difference between an anti-hero and a flawed hero.

Let's just take a moment to clarify the distinct difference between an "anti-hero" and a "villain protagonist". An anti-hero behaves out of a sense of injustice, entitlement, or hopelessness and has some degree of justification for the way he is, despite knowing he's doing wrong. But it's to serve his own goals and purposes. On the other hand, the "villain protagonist" is out to destroy the would-be hero. He doesn't just make poor choices as he tries to cope with life; he's bent on destruction.

Why would an audience be able to sympathize with a character who makes choices we don't agree with, such as in the case with an anti-hero? Aside from the fact that anti-heroes can be fascinating, charismatic, or desperate, they're written in a way that draws in the audience's sympathy.

Before we see all the destructive behavior, we're first introduced to his humanity so we can understand him. There's more power in understanding a person than we ever give credit for. There's often a deep wound that has broken something inside of the anti-hero.

Whether we relate to the wound itself, or just the idea of having a deep wound, we're able to understand the motivations of the anti-hero. When we understand a person's wound or attempt to deal with injustice (or perceived injustice), we're able to suspend our judgment and extend our sympathies.

In life, if we put in the time and effort to understand people, we can understand and care for them even if we still disagree with their choices in the end. But we must distinguish between rooting for the person and rooting for their sin. Think of how amazing God must be at this; how patient and loving he is toward sinners. Over and over again, we humans sin. Some of our choices are horribly offensive and destructive, yet he's able to love the sinner while hating the sin.

Sometimes, a writer writes an anti-hero to represent something about society and culture, which then connects with an audience. An anti-hero is good to study in order to understand how we can sympathize with someone while disapproving of their choices at the same time. From a creative perspective, we can understand the complexities of being human.

From a Christian perspective, we can see what happens when a character pursues life without trusting God. If you watch, you'll see that even when the anti-hero believes he has no other choice, there was one. It was a highly undesirable one, but it was there. The reality is that there might be a situation in life where the only righteous option is to accept the undesirable option, including death. For those whose hope is in Jesus, we have no fear in death. Whatever the cost of the righteous choice (pain, loss, humiliation, grief, and even death), we can face it with Jesus.

Think of it this way: The anti-hero is right in his own eyes and in his own strength, listening to a voice bent on his eternal destruction. He pursues his own purpose, serving only himself. He rejects the righteous path set before him in search of creating his own salvation.

An anti-hero makes excuses for his behavior and sets his agenda above morality.

A hero struggles in his flesh, but ultimately submits to the journey and sacrifices his comfort for the sake of his character arc. He comes to a "Yet, not my will be done," moment. His strength is gained through submission to the author's invitation to choose the narrow path.

Now for the good news. Sometimes, the person who appears to be the villain, turns out to actually be the hero's greatest ally in the end. This character has enough discernment to recognize a flaw that contradicts the hero's goal and he's not about to pretend like it doesn't exist. He's not even going to make it easy for the hero to convince him otherwise.

Think about what it's like to raise teenagers at times. I was totally that teen that thought my parents were against me. I thought they just wanted to ruin my fun and hold me back. But as I matured and had my own character arc, I came to realize that they wanted me to have an incredibly full life, but also that they had the wisdom to see the path I was on and where it was headed.

Some characters are the gatekeeper. Eric Edson talks about a variety of film character types in his book The Story Solution. His explanations of the character types have been very beneficial for me in understanding how to write various roles because each character type comes with its own responsibilities and motivations. The gatekeeper's job is to keep the hero at a distance and refuse to embrace them until the hero has proven himself worthy. But after that, the gatekeeper embraces him and becomes his greatest ally. Think about fathers when their daughters bring a guy home.

```
EXT. FRONT DOOR - DAY

The father stands in the doorway, preventing the new
boyfriend from entering.

                    FATHER
          I don't like him.

                    DAUGHTER
          But Daddy, I love him.

                    BOYFRIEND
          I love your daughter, sir.

The father narrows his eyes and GROWLS under his
breath.

                    FATHER
          We'll see.
```

As the story progresses, hilarity ensues as the father sabotages the boyfriend's attempts to get close to his daughter. This isn't one of my screenplays, but there are several movies like this out there because this is a common scenario. Fathers are protective of their daughters and boyfriends need to prove themselves worthy of their little girl. But after the guy proves himself, the father gives them his blessing. The father is not an adversary, he's a gatekeeper.

If I were to sum up my reason for including this chapter, aside from adversaries being a huge part of storytelling and the fact that there's an adversary in God's story, it would be to encourage you to think about who you surround yourself with. Eric Edson also states in his book that every character in a movie either helps or hinders the hero along his journey. From a writer's perspective, whether the character's intention is to help or hinder the hero, I can use them both to my advantage to get my hero's attention, but my hero is much better off once he figures out who's sabotaging his life.

Your Author is a master storyteller, but you can help the process by being discerning. Some people might appear to be on your side who aren't. Some people may appear to be against you who aren't. Some people are listening to the voice that's telling them they can be their own god. There may be times when you need to remove people from your life while other times, their job is to stick around and make you uncomfortable enough to move. Prayer is necessary to discern who is who.

Chapter 12
The Hero

Who's story is this anyway?

Most of the time, a movie revolves around one main character in the midst of other characters. These other characters lend to the hero's journey, either to support or challenge their goal. They put pressure on the hero to grow, learn, make a decision, etc. But, just like in life, sometimes, if we're not careful, the hero's story can get hijacked. Let's take a look at why and how a hero could lose their importance and power in their own story, and why it matters.

When I was an immature writer, I'd often create these really unique and interesting side characters, but I'd forget to make sure the hero was also interesting and engaging for my audience. I think part of it was because I would write myself as the hero, and therefore, I thought she was completely normal and right. (When the author and the hero have the same perspective, it's hard to create a perspective for the audience. It's like the hero is writing the story.

For this reason, I suggest for writers not to write themselves into a story until they're able to separate themselves from the character.) I'd end up with a main character that didn't have a lot, or anything, to learn. My other characters would often hijack my story because they had interesting flaws.

While I do think it's important to have interesting and wildly entertaining supporting characters, I have to be careful they don't steal the attention from my hero. I need my hero to drive his own story. Part of why this ended up happening is because I would choose to make the hero (me) be the only normal person in their story. That's when I realized that was how I saw myself. I saw myself as normal and somewhat boring, but everyone else around me seemed a lot more interesting.

But why would I see myself that way? Honestly, "normal" has never been a word people used to describe me. So, then I changed my approach. I could allow my character to "think" they were the most normal person in the room as long as I gave the audience evidence that the hero still had his own issues, flaws and oddities. (By the way,

I'm not the only one who's done this. I've seen it in other writers as well. They write the main character based on themselves and, unless they're an experienced writer, the character falls flat simply because they don't know how to write themselves with the appropriate amount of objectivity.)

Sometimes, a hero has to learn to stand on their own two feet. They start off shy and passive. But the only way to get that kind of character to change into being a leader in their own life is to force them into a situation where they have no one else to defer to. Yikes! That means that they'll end up with the rug pulled out from under them and everything they knew flipped on its head. But if the character is more inclined to give-up than to stand up, then it'll take a really, really big and horrible, "do or die" kind of situation to draw it out of them. Either that or I'll drop that character from the story and create a new one.

Here's an example of what I did with a character who refused to move outside of her comfort zone. That's not to say that I had this stubborn character that I was wondering what to do with. Rather, as both the character and story developed in my brain, I realized that Zarrah would have to have something intense happen, and right away, because Zarrah is very much in denial of her true needs. She was stuck in life because she was refusing to deal with something. So, like a good writer, I set to work on destroying her life in order to help her to rebuild it in a healthier way. Here is the inciting incident scene from *Who is Zarrah?*

INT. PSYCH WARD ZARRAH'S CELL - DAY

Zarrah slowly blinks awake.

In a panic, her eyes open wide as she springs upright.

Bare white walls surround the small room with just a single-sized bed, side table and metal chair. The door has a small window with reinforced glass and is locked from the outside.

                    ZARRAH
          Ian! Ian! Help! Where am I? Ian!

The door begins to open. Zarrah backs into the corner.

DR. IAN, a doctor who appears identical to Zarrah's husband, but is cold and borderline heartless, enters the room.

NURSE GIOVANI, a male nurse who appears identical to her band's singer, but is an old soul without any romanticism in him, files in after Dr. Ian with a blood pressure machine.

                    DR. IAN
          You're safe, Zarrah. Calm down.

                              ZARRAH
                  Ian!

Zarrah jumps into Dr. Ian's arms.

Doctor Ian, clinically distant, CLEARS HIS THROAT and
pries Zarrah off of him.

                              DR. IAN
                  We talked about this. You need to
                  maintain a professional distance.

Zarrah WHIMPERS and sits back down onto the bed.

                              ZARRAH
                  What happened? Where are we? What is
                  this place? How did I get here?

Dr. Ian pulls the chair over and sits across from
her.

Nurse Giovani checks her blood pressure. Zarrah
doesn't notice him as her attention is focused solely
on Dr. Ian.

                              ZARRAH
                  What's going on?
                      (off his white, doctor coat)
                  Why are you dressed like that?

Dr. Ian, ignoring her questions, checks her eyes and
makes notes on a clipboard.

Zarrah notices Nurse Giovani.

                              ZARRAH
                  Giovani? Why are you here? What--
                      (off him checking her blood pressure)
                  What are you doing?

                    NURSE GIOVANI
         (without his French-Canadian accent)
    I'm a nurse, Zarrah. I work here.

                    ZARRAH
    You're a... a what?

                    NURSE GIOVANI
         (off Dr. Ian)
    Her pulse is racing, but no more than
    usual under the circumstances.

Nurse Giovani takes the clipboard and makes a note.

                    ZARRAH
    Stop it! Both of you! This isn't
    funny! Tell me what's going on!

                    DR. IAN
    This part is always difficult, Zarrah.

                    ZARRAH
    Always? Ian, get me out of here!

                    DR. IAN
    You need to calm yourself. Your memory
    won't return when you're all worked up
    like this.

                    ZARRAH
    Memory?

Zarrah's eyes dart between Dr. Ian and Nurse Giovani.

                    ZARRAH
    What happened to my memory? What
    happened to me? What...

Dr. Ian glances at Nurse Giovani and takes a deep
breath like, "here we go again".

                        137

                    DR. IAN
          (off Zarrah)
     What's the last thing you remember?

                    ZARRAH
     Um… we went to Aunty Corina's funeral,
     then we went home. I… I remember
     climbing into bed next to you, and
     then… that's it.

                    DR. IAN
     That never happened. I'm not your
     husband. I'm your doctor.

Zarrah struggles to process his words.

                  NURSE GIOVANI
     You've been coming here, off and on,
     for several years.

                    ZARRAH
     No, I… I've never been here before.
     You shouldn't be here either. You're a
     singer, not a nurse.

                  NURSE GIOVANI
     A singer?

                    ZARRAH
     Jazz. You're one of the best… Where's
     your accent? Why are you talking like
     that?
          (off Ian)
     And you're not a doctor, you're my
     husband. We were married on a beach in
     Thailand three and a half years ago.

                    DR. IAN
     You'll get through this easier, and
     remember faster, if you just...

                    ZARRAH
     My memory is fine, dear! Last month, I
     had a tour—
               (off Nurse Giovani)
     WE had a tour of sold-out shows.

Dr. Ian and Nurse Giovani exchange knowing looks and
begin to subtly back away.

                    ZARRAH
     What? So, you're not my husband,
     you're not a singer and I'm not… Not
     what, a musician?
               (off their stares)
     That's ludicrous! Get me a piano, I'll
     prove it to you! I'll play anything
     you want. Kirkland, Pearson,
     Tristano... I'll play Mozart if you
     want.

                    DR. IAN
     Zarrah, do you see the hole in the
     wall behind me?

Zarrah looks past Doctor Ian to see the fist-sized
hole.

                    DR. IAN
     That's what happened last night.

                    ZARRAH
     I don't understand.

                    NURSE GIOVANI
     Your hand, Zarrah.

Zarrah looks down at her hand to see it bandaged with
dried blood spots.

                       139

                    ZARRAH
          (hysterical)
     No! No, my hands are my life. I can't
     play if I'm injured. What did you do
     to me?

Zarrah stands abruptly and Dr. Ian quickly steps back
as if expecting to get hit. She doesn't notice.

Zarrah begins to pace.

                    ZARRAH
     N-n-no. This can't be... I'd never...
     My hands! I don't... I didn't do it.
     No, no, no, no, no...

Dr. Ian nods at Nurse Giovani and he preps a needle.

                    ZARRAH
     None of this makes any sense. This
     isn't right.

Zarrah lunges at the door and tries to open it but
Dr. Ian prevents her from leaving.

                    ZARRAH
     I don't understand! I didn't...

Zarrah grasps at Dr. Ian's face, desperately
pleading.

                    ZARRAH
     Let's go home. I want to go home.

Nurse Giovani sinks the needle into Zarrah's thigh.

She spins around, a myriad of confused emotions in
her eyes.

                    ZARRAH
     What... what did you do to me?

Nurse Giovani cautiously holds the syringe out of her reach.

She turns back to Dr. Ian to see his distant look.

The room spins as Zarrah's eyes blink with heaviness.

                    ZARRAH
          What did you... do? Wha...

Zarrah's head swoons and her eyes close.

When a hero is underdeveloped, they're shallow. There's very little to them. These kinds of characters might work in a sitcom because we've got only a short time to tell a story, it's supposed to be light, and we want the audience to be able to digest everything without much work.

But in a drama or feature, it's a lot harder to tell a compelling story with a shallow, underdeveloped character. (And to be honest, even in a sitcom, we want the audience to eventually see a deeper side to our characters. We give them character arcs throughout a season instead of per episode.) If you think about it, it's hard to sustain interest in a one dimensional character for very long.

All this to say... If you want your Author to take you on greater adventures, seek depth. Learn, experience things, push yourself outside of your comfort zone. If you don't push yourself out of your comfort zone, he'll push you out of it himself. But a person who's not afraid to be himself, is willing to take on risks and challenges, and do new things is a really fun character to work with. This will grab the Author's attention.

The Bible says in 2 Chronicles 16:9 that the eyes of the Lord look for someone on earth through whom he can express his strength (paraphrased). God is looking for someone to express his strength through on the earth. How do we show God, our Author, that we're able to be that man or woman? We have to be willing to trust him as the Author and show ourselves to be a teachable, moldable, and courageous character.

This doesn't mean that you'll stop being afraid, anxious, or whatever other emotions you might have. It means you'll push through them for the sake of the story; the greater calling on your life. I doubt Corrie Tenboom ever once took a cavalier attitude toward breaking the rules to save Jewish lives during WW2. She knew everyday that she could get caught and that it could all be over. But despite the constant threat of danger, she and the people in her home were able to find joy in the midst of it. Until one day, they were caught and she was taken to a concentration camp. But even there, she took risks and pushed through difficult emotions to make choices that were in line with the story her

Author wanted to tell through her life. For me, when my characters make those difficult decisions despite fear and insecurity, I gain a deeper respect for them. That's exactly what a writer hopes his heroes will choose to do. I'm pretty sure that God had respect for Corey's choices during that season of her life. He knew exactly which emotions she was feeling and overcoming. It's important to remember that emotions are an integral part of life, they can bring richness and warn us to pay attention, but they do not need to dictate our decisions.

If the hero is non-responsive to the process or is "already perfect", then he prevents the author from being able to create a character arc. If the problems with the hero's life are always because of the people around them, then they'll cease being the leader. They might play a leadership role within their character, but they won't play the lead of the story itself. Everyone else in the story will have character arcs, but they won't.

Sometimes, these kinds of stories can work, but they're rare for a reason. We want to see a hero struggle, learn, and grow. It's not easy to write a story where the main character is static.

Some people might think that Jesus was a static character from the beginning to the end. But let's think about that for a moment. Jesus was sinless, but not without struggle and temptation. We know this because in Matthew chapter 4, we can read about him being tempted.

The other realities that are not specifically mentioned, but we can easily consider, is that he was a child that went through puberty just like every other human. Those hormones can create a lot of emotional turmoil, temptations, and insecurities. He may have felt the pressure from within his community to get married. It was very common within his culture for a man to get married and have a family. He may have even wanted that for himself but understood that it wouldn't be fair.

We can only surmise why he didn't have a wife and children, but it doesn't seem to say that he wasn't allowed to. He may have had to make a difficult decision; yet one more sacrifice for the sake of his calling. Being that he was fully human and spent his entire life surrounded by people, many of whom spread rumors about him, he was faced with very real challenges that he had to struggle through.

He was sinless. Yes. And in the end, it all added up to providing the ultimate sacrifice. He didn't effortlessly achieve a sinless life and a willing heart. From his youth to his ultimate trial, he was forced to pick up his cross daily and remain in constant submission to the Author.

Lastly, a common way that a hero's story gets hijacked, is because there are too many subplots. Too much going on means they're pulled in too many directions to be able to give any real attention to any one of them. Life comes with a variety of seasons and events. Some people focus on just one thing in life which can create a narrow vision.

While many people will look at that kind of a life like it's missing balance and that it's not well-rounded, it's this group of people that typically accomplish something amazing, like new inventions. They dedicate their whole life to one thing. They may have nothing, or nearly nothing else, going for them, but they're able to achieve something beyond most people's imaginations due to their dedication.

Most people choose to include variety in their lives; family, hobbies, career, travel, social gatherings, etc. This comes with its own benefits. But when a person's schedule is overwhelmed with too many interests and activities, they can't advance their skill in any of them very far.

I've always been a highly motivated person. When I wanted to do something or learn something, I didn't wait for an opportunity to come to me, I'd go find one or make it myself. Between the ages of 7 and 17, I didn't just learn how to play piano, I learned to play every instrument I could get my hands on. At school, I played the French horn, trumpet, trombone (bass clef), and baritone saxophone. At church, I played trumpet, cornet, euphonium, baritone horn, and trombone (treble clef). At home, I played piano. I had some fun on occasion with the bass guitar, drums, and marimba. I loved music. I threw myself into it as a singer/songwriter, as well. I also loved performing, not just music, but acting. Anything that would put me on a stage, I was all over it. I knew that it would be an important part of my life.

I also knew that I wanted to have children. I loved children, even from a young age. Despite being a total tomboy, I always wanted to be a mother. In my teens, as I was considering my future plans, I decided that I wanted to be a mom and I wanted to pursue a career in the performing arts, but not at the same time. I wanted to give myself the freedom to be all-in with each of them and my response to that was to give each its own season in my life. If I tried to do what I'm doing now while I was raising my children, it would've been too much for me. I did continue with the arts as a hobby. I wrote songs and scripts in my own time, but it worked around my life as a mother. And I didn't sacrifice time or resources to pursue the arts as a career. Some people are able to do both without dropping the ball. But, for me, I'm happy with the decision I made and I'm pleased with the result. My sons were able to see me have a dream that I never gave up on, yet waited patiently to pursue it without getting bitter or resentful.

This is an example of my own life and I'm not suggesting that this is the way that every person should plan their life. But I am suggesting that you plan your life. What do you really want to do? What can you let go of? What can you set aside for a different season? Is there a way to provide more opportunity to focus on what really matters in the season you're in?

One of the things I did when my kids were little was to get rid of cable. I realized I was watching too much television and that I had a lot of goals and watching television wasn't helping me achieve them. Truth be told, I think I was a bit addicted to it. I have to say that raising my boys without television was one of the best decisions I made as a parent.

I realize the irony in this, being that I'm a screenwriter, but what I'm really saying is that entertainment is something that must be controlled. It felt hypocritical of me to only celebrate other people's creativity and not fully pursue my own. It might seem like cutting out television wouldn't make that much difference, but think about how much you watch. Even if it's just one hour per day, think about what you could accomplish if you dedicated even just one hour per day to your own goals. By the end of the year, that'd be 365 hours.

I realize that the two topics in this chapter, take courage and don't get distracted, might seem distinct and odd to pair together, but they both aim for the same target. In order to move your story forward and not get hijacked, it'll require both discomfort and discipline. The people who make it are the ones who make it happen. God can part the sea, but we need to walk through it to get to the other side.

Chapter 13
6 Insights the Business and Craft of Screenwriting Taught Me

"I'll be happy when..." is a big fat lie.

In addition to learning some valuable insights from the craft of screenwriting, I've also learned some valuable insights from the business side. **The first of which is that every step of the process is valid and necessary**. If you're in the filmmaking industry, then you know that nothing happens quickly.

The stages of creating a film include development, pre-production, production, post-production, marketing and distribution. You can't be upset that you're not in distribution when you're still in development. It's easy to get impatient and feel like you should be further along than you are, or have the belief that you'll be content once you get to the next stage. But each stage has its own struggle that you could easily find yourself discontent with.

Besides that, eventually, once you reach your goal, you'll just set a new one anyway and start the cycle over. At what point will you enjoy your work? Contentment is a choice. The thrill of the arrival lasts only a short time. Why not learn to enjoy the process at every stage. Since each step leads to the next, you're exactly where you're supposed to be. Progress is progress, no matter how small. Struggle is par for the course. If you are moving forward, you're doing it. Don't cheat yourself out of enjoying the process just because you haven't finished yet. Live in the moment while you work for the future.

Not everything is my job. One of the things I had to learn that is specific to screenwriting is that it's a group effort. Sure, I write the story, develop the plot and characters, and write the dialogue, etc. But what people wear, do with their hair, or how things are decorated, are, for the vast majority of the time, not my business. Unless something actually affects the plot, I'm not allowed to comment on these things. I'm not allowed to cast, direct, create wardrobe, or do the set designer's job. I might have a very specific vision for all of these things, but it's not my place to write them into the script.

Life is much the same way. I might have ideas about the choices other people make about their physical appearance or how to decorate and express themselves, but unless it affects some greater purpose that requires my opinion to be voiced, I need to stay out of it. There are a lot of things that aren't my business to comment on.

As I learned this skill as a screenwriter of how to discern where and when my opinion is welcomed or not, it flowed into my real life. Sometimes, my opinions are relevant, but other times, they're just judgements that have no place in the story. Learning to discern this in real life is incredibly freeing and beneficial.

To everything, there is a time. A season for every purpose under the sun.
Ecclesiastes 3

I would never edit the Bible, but if I did, I would add: **A time to overlook details and a time to micromanage them.**

Writing is rewriting. Do it. Be prepared to redo it. As you improve your skills, you'll have a better first draft. But you'll still have to rewrite it. That's what it takes to have a script worth producing.

However, during the process of creating something, it's important to know when it's the right time to have strict attention to detail. There's definitely a time for perfectionism and micromanagement. But if you do it out of it's right time, it'll frustrate and stall your project. For creativity, you have to start with the big picture and gradually refine the details. If you focus on the minor details during the idea phase, you'll get caught in the weeds and it'll be hard to get started. However, if you neglect to address those minor details later on, you'll end up with a sloppy project. The details absolutely matter, but it's important to have the discernment to know when it's the time and season to be visionary or nitpicky.

Get feedback. Anyone who's gained success at what they do will tell you that getting feedback along the way was part of the process. This is what will make the difference between a hobby and a career. If you want to enjoy what you do without criticism, then keep it as a hobby and do whatever you like with it. There's no shame or judgment in that. But if you plan to make a career of it, prepare yourself for criticism, it's the best way to grow.

Screenwriting was a hobby of mine for over 20 years. But when I decided I wanted to pursue screenwriting as a career, the first thing I did was to find a mentor. In the beginning of working with him, he wanted to get a sense of my writing style, so I would give him a script, then meet with him so he could give me feedback on it.

One of my scripts, I was particularly excited about. It had everything in it. Humor, suspense, drama, and something for everyone. When I met with him, so he could tell me how amazing it was, I knew he'd also have some constructive feedback for me. It was the first draft, after all. I sat down across from him and watched as he pulled out my fabulously written 98 page script. He looked at me... at the script... then exhaled very heavily. "Don't ever show this to anyone," he said. He didn't say it like he was excited and wanted me to protect it. He said it like it could potentially ruin my career before it even got started!

It's definitely not what a writer wants to hear, but I couldn't help but burst into laughter. (He was probably relieved at that.) I thought it was hilarious and I knew I'd tell the story one day. It didn't turn me off. It just revealed to me that I still had a lot to learn.

He went on to ask me who the main character was, what genre it was, and other should-be obvious things. And the crazy thing was that whenever I answered, he looked at me shocked. Apparently, I didn't do a good job with any of it. He told me I had too much going on and it could probably be broken up into 3 different movies.

I didn't always have such a positive attitude to feedback, though. Sometimes, I got really frustrated by it and questioned whether I was wasting my time and effort trying to learn a skill that seemed to elude me. It took a long time for me to understand story structure.

My mentor kept telling me that once I understood it, I'd be unstoppable, but I just couldn't seem to grasp it. I felt like Don in the Kids In the Hall sketch "A Little Something" where he has food on his face and his employee tries to help him brush it off. Don keeps trying to wipe the food off his face, but every time, it's still there. Over and over and over, he tries everything he can think of to clean his face. But he just can't seem to get the cucumber out of his mustache! That was me learning story structure.

"You've got a little issue with your story structure," my mentor, Ned, would say.

"Oh... okay, how about now?" I'd say with the next draft.

"No. No, it's still there."

"How about now?"

"Nope."

"Now?"

"Sorry, no."

"Oh, I know what the problem is." I thought I'd figured it out, so I made a few changes and brought it back. "Here."

"Nope, still there."

"For crying out loud!" I'd go off and do an entire rewrite and come back, "Now?"

"Yeah, still no."

Ugh! It was grueling! I literally cried and asked God why I loved writing so much if I was so bad at it. Thankfully, I had enough sense to know I was just throwing a tantrum and that the people that succeed are the people that don't give up.

Whenever I'd get to this level of frustration, I'd take a few days or a week off to calm down then try again. When it finally all clicked, I was like a toddler during a meltdown recovery. I was happy but I was still breathing like I was crying, like I was still working through the emotions. That was a super frustrating journey.

If you're there in your journey now, or if you happen to find yourself there one day, I hope you don't give up. Some things in life come naturally, while others have to be learned. It's just part of the process.

Feedback can be expensive at times, but it doesn't always have to be expensive. When I finish a script, I like to get feedback from non-writers also. If they can't follow my story, then I clearly missed something somewhere. My point is that you don't have to spend a huge amount of money for feedback, not at the beginning anyway, to find something valuable to learn. I have various tiers of feedback.

In the beginning, I ask my friends and family to read it and let me know their thoughts. These people are my intended audience, so their opinions matter. They're not going to talk to me about formatting or structure, they're just going to tell me what they liked, didn't like, or what confused them or came out of nowhere. Then I can figure out how to address those issues.

After that step, I have peer screenwriters that I send it to. I offer them the same in exchange, so it's a nice trade. It saves money and we're able to give each other really valuable insights. Then I submit it to a more experienced professional, which of course, I pay for.

All of the above paragraphs can easily be applied to my own personal life and growth. My friends and family are who I want to spend time with. If they pick up on something that's off track in my life, I want to pay attention to it. They might be able to shed light on something without me having to spend a bunch of money on it.

However, if there's still something that needs work, I can engage with someone with a greater level of awareness, all the way up to hiring a professional mentor, consultant, or counselor. Which brings me to my next insight. But to have fun while making my point, I wrote this sketch specifically for this chapter. I call it "Throw Money at It".

INT. OFFICE - DAY

An expensively dressed man, MR. KNOW-IT-ALL (50), arrogant and entitled, enters.

He looks around at the business diplomas on the wall and smiles, satisfied.

He approaches DANNY (30), hard-working receptionist.

                    MR. KNOW-IT-ALL
          Hello, may I ask how much for the
          highest level you offer?

                    DANNY
          Our two-year VIP mentorship program?
          We guarantee that if you implement our
          strategies, you'll--

                    MR. KNOW-IT-ALL
          No, the one above that?

                    DANNY
          I'm not sure what you mean. That's our
          highest level.

                    MR. KNOW-IT-ALL
          The work-free program. I want to pay
          for both the knowledge and experience.

Danny stares at Mr. Know-it-all confused.

Mr. Know it all smiles smugly.

                    MR. KNOW-IT-ALL
          Money's no object.

                    DANNY
          You want to pay for two years worth of
          knowledge and experience?

                    MR. KNOW-IT-ALL
          Yes, exactly. I don't have the time or
          desire to spend two years of my life
          learning. I'd rather just pay the
          price and arrive at my goal.

                    DANNY
          But, that's what it takes. A business
          doesn't just become successful
          overnight and there's a lot to learn
          and figure out along the way.

                         153

Mr. Know-it-all starts pulling $100 bills out of his wallet.

                    MR. KNOW-IT-ALL
          How about now?

                    DANNY
          Sir, how would we even transfer the
          knowledge into your head? Or the
          experience...

                    MR. KNOW-IT-ALL
          Well, that's what I'm paying you for
          now, isn't it?

                    DANNY
          Sir...

He pulls out his checkbook and starts writing.

                    MR. KNOW-IT-ALL
          Will $30,000 do it?

He hands Danny the check.

Danny stares at it at a loss for words.

                    MR. KNOW-IT-ALL
          Of course, I'll expect a guarantee
          with that. I need my business up and
          running, and top of its game by
          tomorrow.

                    DANNY
          Tomorrow? Look, we can't guarantee
          something like that?

He pulls his checkbook out again.

                    MR. KNOW-IT-ALL
          My, my, you do drive a hard bargain.

He writes a check and hands it to her.

She GASPS.

                    DANNY
          $100,000?

                    MR. KNOW-IT-ALL
          No price too high to reach my goal.

                    DANNY
          Listen... Most people take a hit for
          the first year or two. Why don't you
          just join the program and save your
          money. The program's only $20,000. You
          could use this other money to live off
          of and build your business full time.
          You're actually in a great position
          to--

                    MR. KNOW-IT-ALL
          I heard your program was the best, but
          I see now that it's a scam.

                    DANNY
          A scam?

                    MR. KNOW-IT-ALL
          Just like all the others. Do you know
          how many programs I've bought and I
          still don't have a successful
          business?

                    DANNY
          I can only imagine.

                    MR. KNOW-IT-ALL
          Well, then.

Mr. Know-it-all snatches the checks back and stalks
out of the office.

Throwing money at a skill doesn't guarantee you'll learn it. That's not to say that paying for education or training isn't a good idea. It's highly valuable. But if you don't put the work in, buying another program won't magically make it sink in.

A lot of the time, you can learn for free. I've always enjoyed learning things that I enjoy learning. That might seem obvious, but think about it. I didn't enjoy learning science in school because I didn't enjoy the subject. But I so loved music, that I would borrow an instrument and a "how to" book for a weekend, lock myself in my room, and figure it out. I learned Spanish by reading a Spanish English dictionary and hanging out with friends who spoke only Spanish.

In my early 20's I decided I wanted to write my first movie, so I started to research online how to format a screenplay. I didn't spend much, if any, money on learning these skills. I just put the time and effort in. That is, until I started working with a screenwriting mentor, then I put the money in as well because that was the level I needed in order to get where I wanted to go. But if I hadn't also put in that same level of passion and effort, I wouldn't be where I am today. I'd still be stuck trying to get the cucumber out of my mustache.

All this to say, be smart about your approach so you don't spend a lot of money unnecessarily. Start with free feedback. It's not as valuable as what you'll pay for, but you can deal with the simple details first.

When it comes to advancing in business, I like to play Jenga. What I mean by that is that I approach it with 2 things in mind. One, I need to find what's willing to move. And two, I need to pay attention to the peripheral details while I pursue it. Years ago, I started voice acting. I was also still raising my family and working toward screenwriting, so

I had a lot going on. But I wanted the experience, I enjoyed it, and we needed some money.

I poked around at the various opportunities and it turned out that audiobooks moved easily. I started to audition and got jobs right away. In time, I recorded 13 audiobooks. I could've pursued commercial or animation, but what I realized when I went to audition for them, is that it often required me to go to a studio to record. For the audiobooks, I could record them in my own home studio, which meant I could work around my family's schedule. But for the other projects, I couldn't.

This is the peripheral aspect. If I'd done those jobs, I would've had to manage a bunch of other schedules around mine. For me, it was a much better choice to manage my schedule around everyone else's. The other jobs paid better, but I probably would've burnt out quickly and it would've been more stressful than it was worth in the end.

If you've enjoyed my short list in this chapter, I encourage you to do a study on business principles in the Bible. I firmly believe that as we put them into practice, and live according to God's instructions, we can become the head and not the tail. (Deuteronomy 28:13)

Another amazing thing about our Creator is that he didn't just set creation in motion and step away. He made sure to provide us with wise instructions. He even told us what would happen if we followed them and what would happen if we didn't, then gave us the choice. My small contribution here isn't even a drop in the bucket of what you can glean from the Word of God.

Chapter 14
How to Be a Hero

Since you are lukewarm, neither hot nor cold, I will spit you out of my mouth. (Some translations even say "vomit".) Revelation 3:16

In case I still have not convinced you to take on the challenge of becoming an active hero, let me share with you what happens when the main character refuses to engage: I get notes back that the hero is passive, i.e. boring and useless.

A passive hero has very little control over how his story develops. He's nothing more than a victim of circumstances. Weak. Not compelling. Uninspiring. The absolute worst thing a writer can do, the thing that leaves the story dead in the water, is to feature a passive character.

An audience would rather watch someone make big mistakes and be wrong, and have to learn the hard way, than for him to do nothing. Why? Because we respect passion, perseverance, and persistence. (Apparently, so does God.) Struggle is part of the human experience. People that avoid it are choosing to be a victim of their circumstances, rather than the hero of their own story.

You might be thinking, "But, I'm not a victim." Maybe not, but if you're not taking responsibility for your own journey, you're letting others determine it for you.

Here's the thing... you're not a guest in your own life. Be active. Make decisions. Drive your own story forward. If you choose wrong, your Author will help you get back on track. But if you refuse to move forward, there are only two possible outcomes. Either your Author will create a situation to force you to move, or your story/calling will be passed on to someone else who will steward it better. Make no mistake, the Author will write his story with or without your cooperation.

If I could speak directly to my hero, I'd say, "Pay attention when things go wrong or upset you, especially when it's something outside of your control. I'm trying to get you to open your eyes and see something."

As I already stated, you don't know your own capacity until it's tested. And in order to test it, you'll have to go through a series of plot points which will create twists and turns in your story. You may decide I'm crazy with this next bit, but I have a theory about life and plot points. I theorize that you can actually begin to recognize plot points in your own life. Once you're able to do that, you can better respond to them. The plot points in a screenplay don't just dictate what happens next, it actually sends the story into the next leg of the journey.

Track with me for a bit. A typical movie follows a Three Act structure. Act One is about context. As the story begins to unfold, the writer will also be sure to include any necessary and relevant information for the audience to understand. The specific character flaw will be revealed or foreshadowed.

Act Two sends the hero off on a journey of discovery. This is when my hero fails the most. It makes sense if you think about it. Approaching anything for the first time is going to come with a learning curve. Since this journey has purpose and will specifically call out his flaw, it's going to pretty much suck for the hero for a while. If he were able to step back and humbly assess what's going on, he'd see that he has the opportunity to learn valuable lessons.

But unfortunately, that's not typically how people respond when they're in the throws of life. And since I can't break the fourth wall and talk directly to him, I have to send him specific people to help show him the ropes.

These characters are in his life for a season and a reason. Without them, he'd flounder. They'll help my hero to learn the new world, but also to learn the principles necessary to achieve his arc. By about half way through this act, he'll finally start to catch on to this new world, but then comes the midpoint; a major plot point.

Now, stick with me because this is where the twists and turns really start to happen. The midpoint looks different in every movie, but it's always there. Something happens that changes everything. Sometimes, it's a massive defeat, sometimes it's a revelation, or a variety of other things.

The point is that there's a moment in the middle of the journey that signals a new path and that life is about to get very real. Suddenly, the tough times the hero went through to learn some new skills or insights feel like child's play. This is where the parallel journey that I took him on converges with the real story he wasn't ready to face before now. In response to this revelation, the hero takes a step toward his goal that now means more than ever. And then... BOOM! Obstacle! (We screenwriters don't like to waste time.)

The second half of Act Two is when the hero faces challenges that point back to what he learned in the first half, but now that there's deeper meaning and higher stakes, it's a lot harder. The highs are higher and the lows are lower.

And that's the reality of life. It doesn't get easier as we grow, it gets harder, because it gets deeper and more meaningful. And sometimes, the hero has to face this part of the journey without their mentor. And just when it appears like maybe he's got a handle on things, Bam! The rug is pulled out from under him. The adversary plays the ace he was hiding up his sleeve. The hero is knocked down so hard that we wonder if he'll get back up.

The crisis moment is the hardest part of the journey. But it's also the most critical. Everything else has led up to this moment. This is the crossroads. This is the test of wills. Will the hero give up? Or will the hero stand up? The hero is often alone at this point, which is a pretty accurate reflection of how we feel in life when we're at our rock bottom. It's one thing to feel like giving up when you've got someone by your side who believes in you. It's an entirely different feeling to be ready to give up and have no one to encourage you.

This is the beginning of the big test. The hero will long for the simplicity of their Act One life. But he's no longer the person he was back in Act One. Too much has happened. And now, here he is at a crossroads. A decision must be made in response to this crisis. The hero's arc hinges on this moment.

In Act Three, we get to see the outcome of the character's response to the question of wills during the crisis. And we get to see the culmination of the external journey. Our hero will either rise to the occasion, even if it means facing a "do or die" situation, or cower to the weight of the dark side and embrace their flaw on a deeper level. Either way, the journey is real, the struggle is real, and the transformation is real.

Now, let's consider the formula of this hero's journey to life itself. In the beginning, you're headed for a test; a crossroads you're not in the least bit prepared for or even aware of. But when you trust that the Author of your life is on your side, that he knows you better than you know yourself, and that he is fully invested in getting you ready for the test ahead, you can stop freaking out so much when life throws you curveballs. Those interruptions and struggles are actually part of the process.

So, about my theory... Ask yourself if the current struggles you're facing is something you'll laugh at later. If so, you're probably in the first half of the journey. Your job at this point is to learn as much as you possibly can. There will actually be something very specific to learn.

I like to pray for wisdom when I find myself in this season. I know I'm failing because of something I'm missing. Thus, I ask my Author, "What am I missing? What am I supposed to learn here?"

The most important piece of this process, though, in order to actually gain the insight I'm asking for, is to ask it with the right attitude. I can only receive an answer if I'm willing to hear it. I might still be frustrated with my situation, but if I'm able to humble myself and ask in a way that doesn't accuse my Author of carelessly ruining my life, then I'm actually able to gain wisdom throughout the days that follow. That wisdom comes from opening my eyes and paying attention to more things happening around me. The Author will put people in my path to speak to me. Or sometimes, I'll see something that stands out to me and I'll investigate it to discover some kind of parallel to my life. But that's me.

The Creator knows how to communicate with me because he knows me. I once watched an entire TV series of a show I actually didn't like because there was something about the main character that I saw in myself. She was always irritated and unhappy (and so was I at that point in my life) and I wanted to understand what made her that way. I realized that she was causing her own misery. Her attitude and refusal to forgive people who'd wronged her in the past was holding her in this constant cycle of drama.

With a heavy sigh, I realized that was exactly what I was doing, too. I had to watch the whole thing to see what lessons her author was teaching her. Maybe I could learn them faster by embracing them without having to fail so hard in my own life. The reason why stories resonate is because the human experience, while unique to each individual, shares a lot of similarities.

Watch for when the journey shifts and becomes more serious. This is the midpoint. But it doesn't necessarily line up with the timeline in life. For example, I'm not saying that if your learning takes six months, this midpoint happens three months into it. But rather like a curriculum, where maybe you spent four and half months on the first half of the curriculum and then the last half of it takes one and a half months. Or vice versa.

There's flexibility in the process of learning and you get to choose to learn at your own pace for a time. (Which is great news because if you get on board with the learning process you can get the work done faster. No need to drag it out.) Here, at the midpoint, is when things start to heat up. The stakes are raised. Your struggles at this point are not likely to be something you look back on and laugh at, but rather, "Thank God, I made it!" The midpoint launches the part of the journey that really matters. Your decisions from here onward could have lasting consequences.

If you have the awareness during the second half of Act two, you could think back to lessons you might've learned lately and see if there are any transferable skills to glean from. At this point, you might want to ask your Author, "Show me what skill and attitude I need to approach this." And then be prepared to get a really annoying answer. It's going to be something you feel like you're still not any good at and that you're not prepared for. He'll ask you to press into something you have little to zero confidence with. However, if you're honest with yourself, you do have the skills to do it, you just haven't done it for something that really mattered yet. For example, working with kindergarteners and working with inmates is nothing alike... except that it is.

When I took on a job teaching life skills at a prison, I was completely out of my element. (You can see this portrayed in my movie Solitary Refinement which is based on the true story of that part of my life.) While I was there, I realized that the skills I acquired while volunteering in my son's kindergarten class were what I needed to manage a room full of unruly, disrespectful inmates.

I had already learned how to confidently walk in authority without being intimidated while I was working with children. I learned how to listen, discern, and defuse arguments, and how to manage the class without being bossy or controlling. These were incredibly valuable skills for when I got a job teaching life skills in a prison.

My students, the inmates, only wanted to be in my class to get a change of scenery and maybe to tell a judge that they're trying to improve their lives. I was extremely intimidated by the job, but probably not for the reason you're thinking. Most people assume that I was intimidated because I was working with hardened criminals. But the truth is that I felt like I had nothing of value to offer them. I was a struggling single mother; I could barely keep up with my own bills and responsibilities. Who was I to try to teach anyone about life skills?

What I realized, which is the same thing I had realized on an easier level with the children, is that I have a unique way of looking at life along with a gift of simplifying complex subjects. That's a character trait that my Author built into me and then gave me an opportunity to develop through faith.

One of the biggest lessons I learned was to lead with vulnerability and humility. Vulnerability and humility don't seem very conducive to working with inmates at first. However, it's what made all the difference. They couldn't figure me out. I think they actually perceived my demeanor as confident. If there was anything I completely lacked, it was confidence. (Confidence to teach 5-year olds is different from confidence to teach adults.) But back to the journey.

If you miss recognizing your journey up to this point, you should at least be able to recognize the crisis moment. This is your rock bottom. This is when you have those thoughts of wanting to give up. Maybe you want to run away, end your marriage, consider suicide... whatever your "I give up! I can't do this anymore!" moment looks like, that's your crisis. But when your crisis moment hits, see it for what it is; the moment right before your potential breakthrough.

The Author has already done the work to prepare you for this moment. Now it's up to you to respond. It's your battle of wills. Will you stand up, ready to make the hard choice, which might demand true agonizing sacrifice? Or will you choose to embrace the lie that you can't? It's hard to think clearly at that moment.

If at all possible, find someone mature and clear-headed to talk to who can help you think back to what you might've learned lately and what you might be able to do to complete the learning process. But most of all, remember that you are not alone. You and your Author are on this journey together. And in this moment, you have His full, undivided attention.

You might be thinking that your adversary is too strong. But remember that the adversary is just a character in the story. He might be stronger than the hero, but he's no match for the Author. The adversary is part of the author's design and creation. He might be pure evil, or seemingly impossible to beat, but the author is fully aware of his plans and always has the final say. And if the author believes the hero can overcome, then of course, he can. A good author can make a way where there seemed to be no way. As long as the hero has chosen to step into their calling and their true identity as the hero of their journey, there's nothing that can stop the victory that's been determined.

Therefore, if I'm the main character in my own life story, what better way to achieve my character arc than to constantly be looking for opportunities to learn. Whatever circumstances I face, I ask myself, "What can I learn from this in order to mature?" In the end, when we enter eternity, that's all we have to show for our time here on this earth. Besides, as a firm believer that the Author of my life is highly invested in leading me from glory to glory, I can press forward into the unknown, on a regular basis, with confidence. Does it scare the heck out of me? Of course. But I trust my Author and do my best to pay attention to the details and maintain a teachable attitude.

Your Author is calling you deeper into your identity. That can't happen without struggle and sacrifice. But embrace it, because as the Bible says: "...we rejoice in our sufferings, knowing that suffering produces endurance, and endurance produces character (arcs), and character (arcs) produces hope, and hope does not put us to shame, because God's love has been poured into our hearts through the Holy Spirit who has been given to us." (Romans 5:3-5)

Of course, I added (arc), but does that verse hit you now like never before? Your Author is giving you the keys to your journey; to your character arcs; to finding the depths of your true identity. And you also have the opportunity to have a counselor to guide you along the way. One thing I don't get to have as a screenwriter, is the ability to give my characters my spirit inside of them to help guide them. But God, in his infinite wisdom and power, has created this incredible opportunity so we don't have to figure out our journey all on our own. And in that moment of crisis, the Holy Spirit is our comforter. We may feel alone, but we're not. It may be legitimately agonizing, but the moment will pass.

Everything changes. Nothing stays the same. Seasons come and go. Enjoy what you have when you have it. Learn what you can when you're struggling. And don't give up right before your greatest breakthrough.

Chapter 15
Full Circle

We began with the end, so we'll end with the beginning.

Since I already know the end of my movies, I write the beginning with that in mind. The entire story is set-up within the beginning. All of the necessary information and details will be revealed, but hidden at the same time.

As a writer, I now know how to recognize those details when I watch other movies. I know how to capture that jewel of information that seems like a passing detail in the set-up as the piece that will bring all together in the end. Some people might say that learning how to write a screenplay ruins the magic of watching a movie, and they're not entirely wrong. But what it also does is develop a true appreciation for well-written stories. The same applies in life.

So many of the answers we need will connect to the past. As I mentioned in a previous chapter, we can look back at the patterns in our lives and assess what's really going on. When did that pattern start? Is the cause known?

Since many character flaws developed as a survival mechanism after a wound, then the patterns that stemmed from our childhood are riddled with childish reasoning. If we can recognize that the child version of ourselves did the best they could with what they knew at the time, but that as an adult, we can reason differently, then we can start to change our patterns.

Everything I write as the story plays out lends to the journey of preparing my hero for his final test. With that in mind, I choose when, in his overall story, I want to start this process of preparation. For example, if my hero is going to face a test that requires generosity, then I need to give him enough time to acquire that quality. I'll choose the point in his life in which I deem it appropriate to start this journey, and go from there. Given that I've created the world and the characters, I know exactly when that should be... well, eventually, I know when that should be. Sometimes, it's a few sleepless nights later, but eventually, typically when I stop thinking about it, it becomes clear.

The first thing I do to start their journey is to interject something new into their life. That typically includes messing it up and changing their routine. Do my characters get angry about this sudden change in their life? Most often, yes, very much so. I'm sure if they knew me by name and were able to, they'd curse me to my face.

But the reality is that they don't know there's a test coming. They don't know what it's going to take to get them ready for it. They don't even know what they're supposed to learn, or that they're supposed to be learning something. All they can do is respond to what I place in front of them. And, since I can't speak with them directly, the only way to get their attention is to frustrate their plans in order to convince them to try something different. They'll try to cope in a variety of ways and I'll have to keep frustrating their plans until they choose the path they need to be on; in order to learn and grow; in order to prepare for the test.

But one of the important moments in a movie is the break into Act 2. It's the moment when the hero steps out into their adventure. They've chosen this moment. It's when the beginning becomes the middle.

This moment only happens because the hero has determined to do so. No matter our beginnings, the only way to move into the middle, toward the end, is to step out in faith and determination.

Below is a script that very much reflects a real-life situation, ending with a conversation I had with a teenager years ago. (Names of the people have been changed.) This teen had such severe anxiety that he didn't want to leave his apartment. It took months of spending time with him just to be able to get to the point where we could have a real conversation.

EXT. CARNIVAL FAIR GROUNDS - DAY

CROWDS line-up for rides, play games, and eat mini-donuts.

JACOB, 4, grips his mother's hand as she leads him through the crowd toward an ice-cream vendor.

CLAIR, 30, Jacob's loving mother, releases Jacob's hand to pay for two cones.

She hands one to Jacob and his face light's up.

                    CLAIR
          Come on, let's find a place to enjoy
          these.

Jacob wobbles and Clair saves the cone from toppling.

                    CLAIR
          How about I carry that for you.

Jacob smiles and follows Clair as she starts walking.

Jacob looks around at the chaos and excitement of the fair.

Suddenly, a group of KIDS run past, knocking him over.

Clair doesn't notice and continues walking.
Jacob, not hurt, stands up and keeps walking.

A moment later, he stops and looks around.

He spins around.

                    JACOB
          Mom?

His surroundings swirl around him.

                    JACOB
          Mom!

All the noises around him sound like they're underwater.

Tears fill Jacob's eyes as he frantically spins around, looking for his mother.

                    JACOB
          Mom!

INT. HOME - JACOB'S BEDROOM - MORNING (11 YEARS LATER)

Jacob, now 15, startles awake, his sweaty hair stuck to his head. He works to calm his breathing.

Clair bursts in.

                    CLAIR
          Jacob? Honey? You okay?

Clair sits on the bed and holds him while his breathing settles down.

INT. HOME - KITCHEN - DAY

Jacob eats lunch at the table with Claire and VERN, 40's, Jacob's father.

                    VERN
          (off Jacob)
     You all ready to go?

                    JACOB
     I don't want to go today.

                    VERN
     Which is exactly why you need to.

Jacob slumps deeper into his seat.

                    CLAIR
     I thought you said you liked Becky.

                    JACOB
     It's not about her.

                    VERN
     Just go for an hour. If you feel like
     you want to come home after an hour,
     then come home.

Clair nods encouragingly at Jacob.

INT. CAFE - DAY

Jacob sits at a booth across from BECKY, 30, his attentive tutor. A binder and textbook lay open between them.

                              BECKY
          An adjective describes a noun and an
          adverb describes a verb. Can you give
          me an example of a noun?

Jacob checks his watch.

Becky waits for a moment.

                              BECKY
               (whispers)
          Person, place or thing.

                              JACOB
          Um...

Becky studies Jacob for a moment.

Jacob shrugs and closes his book.

                              BECKY
          We can change subjects if you prefer.

                              JACOB
          Can you call my mom to pick me up now?

Jacob packs up his books. Becky nods and helps him.

INT. CAFE - DAY

Jacob finishes a worksheet and hands it to Becky with
cautious pride.

She checks it over, smiling.

                              BECKY
          Nice!

Jacob smiles.

                              BECKY
          Well, we're done early. Let's go for a
          walk, get a little fresh air.

Jacob starts to pack up.

EXT. STREET - DAY

Jacob and Becky walk along, chatting. Becky sees an
ice-cream truck pulled over.

                              BECKY
          Hey, I'll buy you an ice-cream. A
          celebration for finishing the unit.

MINUTES LATER

They receive their cones from the VENDOR.

                              BECKY
          Truth be told, I've been craving ice-
          cream lately and this is really just
          for me. It just helps me to justify it
          for myself if I say I'm celebrating
          you.

Jacob CHUCKLES.

Jacob wobbles slightly and Becky steadies his hand
with the cone to save it from toppling.

Jacob stares at it.

QUICK FLASHBACK

Clair's hand steadies young Jacob's hand at the fair.

BACK TO SCENE

Jacob freezes and struggles to breathe.

                    BECKY
          Hey, you alright? Look at me. You're
          safe. I'm right here.

Becky's calm, confident words stabilize him.

Jacob takes a deep breath.
Becky watches closely to see that Jacob's anxiety
settles.

                    JACOB
          I just had a memory.

Becky nods, playing it cool.

                    BECKY
          That happens sometimes.

                    JACOB
          Yeah.

They continue walking.

                    BECKY
          Do you want to talk about it?

Becky eats her cone as she walks.

                    JACOB
          When I was little, I got lost at a
          fair.

                    BECKY
          That must've been scary.

                    JACOB
          I was screaming for my mom. It was
          only for a minute or two, but I
          thought I lost her forever.

                    BECKY
          How old were you?

                         JACOB
        Four. It was really loud and I
        couldn't see through the people.

Jacob's eyes well up, but he speaks through it.

BEGIN FLASHBACK

EXT. CARNIVAL FAIR GROUNDS - DAY

Young Jacob spins around frantically.

                    YOUNG JACOB
        Mom!

The surroundings close in on him.

END FLASHBACK

EXT. STREET - BACK TO SCENE

Jacob stops walking and focuses on his breathing.

                         BECKY
        That was a dangerous situation for a 4
        year old. What do you think would be
        different now?

Jacob looks up, confused.

                         JACOB
        What?

                         BECKY
        Well, you're not four anymore. What
        would happen if you were in the same
        situation now? At fifteen?

Jacob thinks about it.

                              BECKY
              Would you know how to get back to the
              car in the parking lot? Or walk home?

Jacob stares at her, still pacing his breathing.

                              BECKY
                    (carefully)
              A four year old doesn't have a lot of
              skills to work with. But you're not
              four anymore.

Wheels turn in Jacob's head.

BEGIN FLASHBACK

EXT. CARNIVAL FAIR GROUNDS - DAY

Young Jacob spins around in a panic, looking for his
mother.

Suddenly, it's 15-year-old Jacob looking around.

He sees his mother walking with the cones.

His face lightens, his panic lifts.

END FLASHBACK

EXT. STREET - BACK TO SCENE

Jacob looks at Becky, a smile peaks through and his
tears are now happy tears.

                              JACOB
              Yeah. Yeah, I could find my way.

Becky offers a soft smile, though it's impossible to
miss the pride and joy behind it.

This teen changed overnight after our conversation. The realization about where his anxiety stemmed from set him free. His childish reasoning was that he never wanted to be lost again and therefore, he hated leaving the house without his mother at his side. But as a 15-year-old, he realized that he had the skills to take care of himself even if he did get lost. His now mature reasoning was able to cancel out his childish reasoning without shaming it. It served its purpose and kept him from being separated from his mother throughout his childhood. But as he moved into his adulthood, it was no longer necessary.

As a writer, I don't just mess up my hero's plans to see what he will do. I mess up specific plans in order to get my character to respond in a specific way. I call him to come on an adventure, although he doesn't always see it that way. This adventure comes with ups and downs, but its ultimate purpose is to point to a flaw that stems from a wound. This is the wound I want to heal.

If you have an undesirable habit that you recognize stems from a childhood trauma, you can reason it out as an adult without shaming your younger self. You can even say, "Thank you for doing your best to protect me. I'll take it from here." It may very well be the key that unlocks your character arc.

This isn't to say that it'll heal the trauma itself, but rather to suggest that it could release you from patterns of unhealthy behavior. The trauma may take longer to heal from, and your inner child might fight to protect you by wanting to keep old patterns of behavior. But like Bill, in the short script Words, you, today, get to make choices for your present and future.

In the chapter on music, I dropped a major bomb about my past; I used to hear demonic voices telling me to harm myself. I couldn't just end this book without addressing that. As I share the rest of this story,

I want you to keep in mind all the things you've learned to this point and see how my Author was writing my story.

I grew-up attending church and always believed that God existed and was good and holy. I understood that it was desirable for God to call you to something meaningful, but as I aged and my sins and failures became adult-sized, I began to question God's ability to call me to anything. I left home at 17 years old and by the time I was 21, I was living with my boyfriend and pregnant. Since I was facing motherhood, I wanted to get my life back on the right track and get right with God. One thing after another, I tried to fix my sins so I could return. But nothing I did seemed to make me feel like I was any closer. Even after our second child was born and we got married, I still felt like God was impossible to reach.

The father of my children had zero interest in, or respect for, God. He would laugh at me if I prayed for a meal. When I wanted to return to church, he would accuse me of abandoning my children if I left them home. And if I took them with me, well... he hated when I took the babies anywhere. He was controlling and isolating, but I didn't see it at the time.

It's hard to say exactly when the voices started because they would masquerade as my own thoughts. They would say things like, "You're not a good mother. Your kids would be better off without you. You're not a good wife. If you die, people will miss you for three months, then move on with life. Nothing is going right. Nothing will ever change. You need relief. Alcohol can make you feel better. Smoking will give you some relief. Wouldn't it be nice to get high? Cutting will release the pain."

On and on, these "thoughts" would speak to me. And several times, my husband at the time would say the same thing or something similar. He'd call me useless and accuse me of being a neglectful mother.

It's no wonder that depression engulfed me the way it did. I began to fanticize about committing suicide. Every time I was driving alone in the car, I'd hear those voices, louder than ever, telling me I was worthless and that the world would be better off without me. I was being isolated from people outside of my home and my pride kept me from opening up to people or reaching out for help.

One night, I was driving home from work and the voices were so loud and convincing that I couldn't think of anything else. As I drove through my tears, the voices getting louder and more chaotic in my mind, I made the decision to swerve left, off the road. The area I was in and the speed I was going provided ample opportunity. But in the brief moment between my brain telling my hands to turn the wheel and my hands receiving the message, a different voice cut through the chaos and cleared away all the other voices. It said, "Your kids would rather you be divorced than dead."

There was silence in my mind for the first time in years. I was able to think clearly. I had never even considered divorce since I believed that I was the problem. I didn't know what was happening, but I knew it was true.

My response was to cry out, "To the One who created me... I've made a mess of my life. Whatever's left of it, it's yours. I'm done doing things my way. Show me you have something better." I had strayed so far from my faith and was so lost that I didn't even know who to cry out to. I know that some people have stories of feeling a weight lift off them when they surrender their lives to God. But that wasn't my story. I didn't feel any different. I drove home, climbed into bed, and wondered what would happen next.

In the days, weeks, and months that followed, I remained in constant prayer. I brought God into every area of my life and decision-making. I didn't have a Bible, so I asked God to speak to me in ways I could understand. I told him I wanted to do things his way, but he needed to show me what that was. I quickly realized that God is able to communicate with us and that his ways were usually the opposite of what I would've done.

I prayed for God to change the heart of my husband, but it seemed that the more I prayed, the harder his heart became. God gave me permission to leave and start a new life. This was not an easy decision as it affected my children as well. But as I continued to surrender to God's will for my life, I grew stronger and my life improved. As I got to know the One who created me, I began to know who he created me to be.

Two years later, I was sharing my testimony with a friend. He helped me to realize that those "thoughts", which I was already referring to as voices that would swirl in my head, were demonic.

That's when I realized that I had never heard them again after that other voice spoke to me and cleared them away. And that's when I realized that it was God who had spoken to me. If I wasn't already sold out and hopelessly in love with God by that time, I was in that moment. As I finally pieced together the journey that my Creator set me on to reveal his love for me specifically, my heart was filled with gratitude that can never be removed. I realized that it broke his heart every time I doubted his love or consideration for me.

When I share this testimony, it feels like the end, because it was the end of my oppression, but in reality, it's the story of my beginning. When I gave my life to my Creator, I meant it with every fiber of my being. I am no longer my own and I am definitely not the enemy's. I have been redeemed from the brink of death.

In a sense, I did die that day. My will had to die so God could raise me to life anew. And what an incredible life he's given me. When I asked him to show me he had something better, I was thinking that he'd help me find peace and stability in order to raise my boys. But He's done far above and beyond anything that that once broken woman could've ever imagined.

Like the incredible Author he is, God sees the big picture. He's in the details, but he doesn't get caught in the weeds. He weaves tension and release throughout our lives by design. He loves to establish cycles and patterns, bringing us to a deeper level of relationship and understanding each time we repeat seasons. He loves to hide himself within our story. And like all great writers, He loves His work. He won't abandon a story he's started. (Philippians 1:6)

Our Author's intent is to take us from glory to glory; arc to arc. As we learn, grow, heal, and overcome, we blossom into our true identity. As we walk out each new normal at the end of a journey, it seamlessly transitions into the beginning.

My advice as a writer, and as a character in God's story, is to make the most of the season you're in, since you won't get to repeat it. Sure, you'll come back around to another season like it, but in order to rise to the next level of maturity in your walk with your Creator, you'll need to make choices and changes. If your old pattern no longer serves you and it's staring you in the face, receive it as a call to adventure. It means your Author wants to work on it with you. You're not in it alone.

Whether we're completing a season, a cycle of seasons, or life itself, it will always end with a new beginning... middle... and end.

Additional Resources

As you continue your journey forward with your Author, I encourage you to check out these additional resources meant to help in guiding your steps!

From now using what you've learned and writing your own stories, to getting connected and inspired by others' stories, we have something for you.

Learn to write your own scripts with the Faith & Family Filmmakers Association Screenwriting Academy: *faffassociation.com*.

Listen to the Faith & Family Filmmakers podcast: *faffpodcast.com*.

Follow Jaclyn for even more stories, insights, and helpful resources at: *jaclynwhitt.com*.

Thank You!

Thank you so much for reading *In the Beginning, Middle, and End*! Especially if you enjoyed it, would you leave your honest review on the book page? It truly helps reach other readers and encourages them to check it out. It can even be just a couple of sentences!

Go to: *amazon.com/dp/B0D9R7XS9V*.

I deeply appreciate your time and support!